The Ultimate 70s Collection

ICONIC MUSICIANS AND ALBUMS
MOVIES THAT DEFINED A GENERATION
LEGENDARY TOYS AND VIDEOGAMES

CONTRIBUTORS
John Romero, Mark Bussler,
Philip Oliver, Jim Bagley,
Gary Bracey, and Trip Hawkins

FOX CHAPEL
PUBLISHING

Articles in this issue are translated or reproduced from *The Ultimate 70s Collection* and are the copyright of or licensed to Future Publishing Limited, a Future plc group company, UK 2022.

Used under license. All rights reserved. This version published by Fox Chapel Publishing Company, Inc., 903 Square Street, Mount Joy, PA 17552.

ISBN 978-1-4971-0378-8

The Cataloging-in-Publication Data is on file with the Library of Congress.

To learn more about the other great books from Fox Chapel Publishing, or to find a retailer near you, call toll-free 800-457-9112 or visit us at *www.FoxChapelPublishing.com*.

We are always looking for talented authors. To submit an idea, please send a brief inquiry to acquisitions@foxchapelpublishing.com.

Printed in China
First printing

The Ultimate 70s Collection

A Letter from the Publisher

Remember the days filled with sore thumbs and hands from chaotically playing Rock 'Em Sock 'Em Robots and Hungry Hippos? Or how about updating your closet to better suit a light-up dancefloor? Personally, I remember the first day I left my portable radio at home for the exciting new Walkman. Within these pages, you'll have a blast rediscovering all the pivotal moments that made the 70s such a significant decade.

During the 70s, we witnessed best-selling movies like *Star Wars*, that was a cinematic breakthrough and monumental shift in the sci-fi genre. What started as a simple tennis game became a revolutionary development and mass phenomenon in the videogame industry, also known as *Pong*. Musical artists like Elton John, Donna Summer, David Bowie, Queen, Fleetwood Mac, and others took the world by storm, changing music forever—from disco, funk, and alternative to rock, punk, and pop.

While this book is a bit different from what we usually publish, it was brought to us by the editors of *Retro Gamer Magazine* and it's with nostalgic excitement that we proudly present it to you. A pivotal time in history, the 70s—following up on the international success of the Beatles—really launched the beginning of mass culture and globalization. The world was introduced to American movies, British games, music, pop culture icons, and more that would forever leave a mark. It's interesting how things had become international and shaped culture around the world ever since. Sounds similar to what happened with the iPhone!

And this is only scraping the surface of what a defining decade the 1970s were. So, sit back and enjoy all the wonders of the 70s! If you remember the era yourself, you may wince, or you may be proud of the things featured within these pages. If you weren't born yet, I hope you have fun learning all the things that came before.

—Alan Giagnocavo, Publisher

CONTENTS

26

76

128

20

44

108

132

The Story of
PONG

It was 47 years ago that a simple warm-up engineering project helped thrust a new industry and company into the public eye, forever changing how we view entertainment and becoming the digital fire for the modern caveman. Take a behind-the-scenes look at the history and influence of Pong

They were at a turning point in their lives. Nolan Bushnell and Ted Dabney couldn't stay with Nutting Associates any more – that much was clear. But what were they supposed to do now to get their two-person game-engineering firm, Syzygy Engineering, out on the market?

Nolan found the answer by cold-calling several of the 'old guard' arcade game firms in Chicago. Bally, which had purchased fellow manufacturer Midway three years before, was interested in their videogame technology, but not if the duo was still attached to Nutting.

Making a calculated decision, they gave notice at Nutting and rented a 2,000 square foot front-end office with back-end garage on Scott Boulevard to start up operations. Incorporating the company as Atari, they signed a contract with Bally to design a pinball machine, an electromechanical arcade game, and a video arcade game. Money from the contract would come in monthly, and combined with a coin-op route of pinball machines they had purchased from a fellow former Nutting employee, the nascent videogame and arcade company had enough to get their small firm up and running and hire some employees.

Their first employee was Cynthia Villanueva, a babysitter for Nolan's

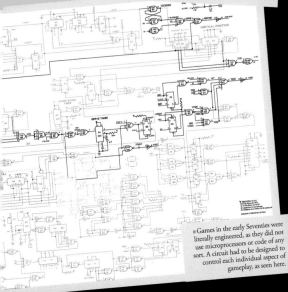

» Games in the early Seventies were literally engineered, as they did not use microprocessors or code of any sort. A circuit had to be designed to control each individual aspect of gameplay, as seen here.

kids who was hired as a combination secretary and work-mother, making sure they'd eat during the long hours at work.

It was the second employee, though, that has the real bearing on this story. Al Alcorn had been part of a stable of interns at Ampex's Videofile division when Nolan and Ted worked there. A burly American football player in high school who decided in college that his future lay in electrical engineering rather than the gridiron, he was on his six-month rotation when he first met Nolan and Ted. By the time they were starting up Syzygy Engineering at the end of May, Nolan paid the associate engineer a call.

"He offered me a salary – about $1,000 a month – and ten percent of the stock in the company," says Al. "I was already making $1,200 a month as an associate engineer and the stock seemed worthless to me because I couldn't care less. It was a nice token, but not that important to me. I accepted the offer because I thought that it would be fun."

Al had never seen a videogame before, and Nolan got him up to speed by plopping the diagrams for his and Ted's game, Computer Space, into his lap. In between looking over the technology, Al also had to pull his weight in the small startup where everyone had a role. Ted's was to build the pinball machine, keep the company's books, manage the facilities, and run the coin-op route. Nolan's job was to be Nolan – look over progress and, as Al puts it, "keep bullshitting" Bally that they were making progress so it would keep sending checks. Al's role, besides engineering, was to help collect the coins on the route that was helping to keep Nolan and Ted afloat, since they weren't making a salary themselves.

"[Collecting the money] taught me about designing things that work in a public environment," Al says. "When a machine steals your money you feel you have a right to destroy it. So it has to be really well built, but still be cheap to manufacture. I learned a lot about that from collecting on the route."

Al's conditions were spartan, consisting of a work area with a single old oscilloscope that they all shared. But the fun he was seeking was just about to really begin.

Pong begins...

It started with a challenge to make a game. Nolan

wanted a driving game but had decided that Al needed to warm up with something simple. So Nolan lied to Al, claiming they had a contract with GE for a consumer videogame that had to use very few chips. Thinking back to the Magnavox Odyssey demo he had been to that past May where he saw a tennis game, he decided to tell Al the game was to be an electronic version of tennis. He then proceeded to describe what he saw of Magnavox's game, aiming to have Al tweak it further.

One thing was clear in Al's mind: he couldn't make heads nor tails of Nolan's unorthodox schematics that he'd been trying to study. Nolan had to walk through the basics of the spot-motion circuitry that Ted had designed, explaining how the sync generators work to draw things on the screen.

Al started out by getting a ball moving around on the screen, designing the circuits needed to change direction. This process shouldn't be lost on the reader, who may be more used to today's gaming world where Pong is commonly used as an intro to game programming. Arcade videogames didn't use microprocessors at this time, so there was no game code. In those days, videogames were engineered – no different to any other consumer product like a toaster, telephone or stereo. Game designers in the early Seventies were electrical engineers like Al; their job was creating a circuit for every mechanic, a fiddly task that would later be done entirely in software.

When Al went to work on the iconic paddle controls for the game, several ideas came rolling out from the creative part of his brain. Ideas that would become an important part of making it the fun game it is to play to this day.

First there was how to do a simpler version of the 'English' Nolan had

PONG MEMORIES

My first memories of Pong are from when my mum got me a Binatone TV Master MK IV in the late Seventies. It was fantastic – you could actually play games on your TV!

It may not look much by today's standards, but it was bloody good fun! So many great memories for a classic game!

Jim Bagley, Ocean Software

HOME-GROWN PONG

A selection of the many Pong variants that were available on the home market

01. Magnavox Odyssey
Ralph Baer's influential console was created in 1972 and featured two hand controllers. It is the first home example of a console featuring a tennis game, and inspired Atari to create *Pong*.

02. Super Pong
Wanting to emulate the success of *Pong* in the home, Atari created Super Pong in 1976. Unlike similar home systems of the time, *Pong* was the only game available on it.

03. Wonder Wizard
General Home Products' Wonder Wizard is an interesting system, as it features a Magnavox Odyssey 300 circuit board in the original Magnavox casing. It features a number of games, including a *Pong*-like version of tennis.

04. Telstar Ranger
The Coleco Telstar Ranger was released in 1977 and is a six-game variant of the original Telstar that was released. It came with an authentic-looking pistol and two controllers, with the gun games being *Target* and *Skeet*.

05. Video System
This system from First Dimension looked interesting, with the first model being released in 1975. The better 1976 variant, which is the one shown here, played relatively complex variants of *Pong*, including an innovative four-player mode.

06. Television Tennis
Does exactly what it says on the tin. This home system was created by a small company called Executive Games and was first released in 1975. It's notable for its chunky design and unusual controllers.

07. Heathkit GD-1380
As with other systems featured here, the Heathkit is powered by a universal chip, in this case the AY-3-8500. It's a bit of an oddity, and not just due to its radio-like appearance. It only works on Heathkit TVs and the audio comes through the TV.

08. Interfab Pong IV Kit
Another interesting model, as it existed in three distinct forms: fully assembled, partly assembled or in kit form, requiring full assembly. Released by Interfab in 1976, it played just two games, Tennis and Handball.

09. VideoSport MK2
This stylish-looking system is one of the earliest European variants of *Pong*, appearing in 1974/1975. Created by British retailer Henry's, it included three games: *Tennis*, *Football* and *Hole In The Wall*.

10. Philips Tele-Spiel
We love the look of this, and not just because of its bright primary colors. It came packed with a *Pong* variant, and four additional games could be purchased. There's no scoring system, meaning players physically score games on the actual controller.

11. Videomaster Home TV Game
Another early European system, believed to have been first available in 1974. It played *Tennis*, *Football* and *Squash* and is notable for having a large number of variants.

12. Binatone
Distinctive thanks to its orange casing, it's another six-game system, possibly based on the same chip as the Telstar Ranger. It also includes two gun games, with the gun peripheral having a cool scope.

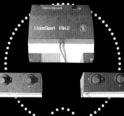

Images courtesy of David Winter. Visit **www.pong-story.com** for more great information about *Pong*.

» Nolan inspecting rows of Pong games being manufactured in 1973 at a roller rink. He and Ted needed the space, and this vacant rink that The Doors had played at several years earlier proved the right fit.

"We cut the numbers to Bally to one third. Bally still thought we had exaggerated the numbers"

described seeing on the Odyssey. Simply a way to make the ball volley off the paddle in unpredictable lines, it makes gameplay between opponents a bit more chaotic, like real tennis. The Odyssey uses a separate 'English' dial control, but Al was able to come up with a simpler method that proved just as fun.

The paddles in *Pong* are 16 pixels high, and by segmenting it into eight sections each, two pixels high, he was able to dictate how the ball angled off the paddle. The catch was, the angles were an illusion created by horizontal and vertical speeds. The horizontal speed was set by how many times a volley occurred between the paddles, a feature that Al had added to make it more interesting.

"Nolan had told me that it had to be a consumer product," he explains, "so I thought two guys could sit there and play it forever if the ball had just one speed. So I added the speed-up where after a certain number of volleys it would go faster and faster."

Whatever segment of the paddle was hit would then decide the vertical speed of the ball. Hitting the top or bottom ones would imbue the ball with the highest speed, with each segment closer to the center decreasing. Finally, the middle two segments produce no vertical speed change. Combined with the variable horizontal speed, players were now able to create a much more unpredictable, entertaining volley.

Another 'feature' that Al added to the game actually spawned from a defect in the design. The motion of the paddles on the screen is controlled by a special timer chip, the 555, which uses the motion of the spinner controllers as part of its control. A limitation in the chip meant the paddles were unable to be drawn all the way to the top of the screen, leaving a small gap that a ball can fit through. Instead of coming up with a fix, Al decided to leave it in as a stalemate breaker. The bug became a feature.

Nolan's demand for a low chip count made Al self-conscious through the coming months of the design process. At every turn and request from Nolan to add additional features, Al kept second-guessing how it could be done. On-screen scoring, an on-screen net instead of one affixed to the TV screen, and then probably the most far-reaching request. When Ted and Nolan came

PONG MEMORIES

Pong was truly the first casual game and the first social game. Everyone played it. I mean, everyone. It is ironic that videogames after *Pong* quickly became too complicated for the mainstream public and that we are only now working our way back to mass-market casual and social games.
Trip Hawkins, founder of Electronic Arts

to Al asking for the sounds of a crowd, something had to give. There just wasn't a budget.

Nolan wanted cheering for scores; Ted wanted boos and hisses for missing a ball. They had to compromise with a blipping sound that's now synonymous with early videogames and instantly identifies *Pong*.

By mid-August of 1972, about three months since he started, Al had completed his 'test game'. Nolan was ready for Al to move on to his 'real project', the driving game they'd actually be providing to Bally. The tennis game would just fade off into the darkness. There was one problem, though: it was too much fun to play. Ted thought the game was a great finished product and should be the one they submitted to Bally, and Nolan wanted no part of that. The two had what Ted described as a "knockdown, drag-out" screaming match in each other's faces. The end result was that Nolan agreed to at least test it out.

Going to Al and presenting it as his idea, Ted offered a plan to test out the game at one of their locations, still not letting on that there was no GE contract. Al agreed, still thinking the product had been a failure based on the cost specs he had been given. Ted got a television monitor ready for it, using the same gutting process he had developed when he first created the spot-motion circuitry for *Computer Space*. He then built a cabinet over the following weekend – a half-sized, boxy design for the television and *Pong* prototype to sit inside.

» By 1973, other companies started entering the market with their own clones of Pong, and the market was soon overflowing. This was an ad Atari ran in Cash Box magazine at the time to help combat what Nolan called "the jackals".

"That's when I said, 'Either we build it ourselves or we go home. I don't want to go home!'"

Painted in a garish red/orange color to attract attention, its size ensured that it would have to be propped up on something to bring it to face level. There were no directions on the control panel, no description of what it was about, nothing. A box with a TV screen, two knobs, and a coin box. There was one thing printed on the metal control panel, though. A single word named after the sound of the game: *Pong*.

They decided to place it at their favorite location out of all of them on their coin-op route: a tavern called Andy Capps. With seven machines there already, they elected to set the Pong prototype on top of a barrel next to Computer Space.

The legend today goes that the machine stopped working because of overflowing coins, but that's not the cause of the first breakdown. The first time was because of cheap potentiometers, the electronic component that the spinners are actually made from. They're usually rated for a certain number of turns, and Al calculated by the quantity of coins in the box that it was getting far more than what it was rated for. Probably about 100,000 turns by the end of the month.

Then, shortly after that, Al got the call for the more famous problem. The owner of Andy Capps called him to say the machine stopped working and that they should come down and fix it because there were lines of people still waiting to play. After heading down and opening the coin box, Al suddenly found an avalanche of quarters flowing out. The only reason the game had stopped working was that the coin mechanism, appropriated for *Pong* from a laundry machine, had overflowed onto the circuit board. A simple fix, but also a promising start.

Nolan and Ted decided to go ahead and build another 12 *Pong* machines in more standard-sized cabinets. Ten would go out to the other locations on the coin-op route, and they'd keep one at the office. The final one would be sent to Bally to evaluate for the fulfillment of the videogame portion of their contract. Yes, Nolan had acquiesced after the success at Andy Capps.

Success and manufacturing

The numbers kept coming in through September and they couldn't believe it. The new *Pong*-filled coin-op route had almost tripled their earnings. Ted was making enough money to look at replacing his old car. This game was going to be a big moneymaker for Bally – if it ever responded.

Nolan kept in contact with Bally, but it was apparent that it was stalling. Ted explains: "We were getting plenty worried because our future was in Bally's hands. We decided to put together an income report to give Bally some incentive. As we put this report on paper, the numbers looked impossible. We knew that they would think that we cooked the books.

"Since the numbers were so damned high, I suggested that we cut the numbers to Bally by one half. The numbers still looked unlikely, so I said that we needed to go to one third. A couple of the machines were much lower than the others, so Nolan suggested that we not cut those ones so drastically. I said that if we're going to lie, we have to be consistent so we would remember what the lie was. He agreed.

"Believe it or not, Bally still thought we had exaggerated the numbers. They were still stalling, but they owned it so we were up a creek. That's when I came up with the idea to get Bally to reject the game."

Nolan, Ted and Al were in Nolan's office, contemplating their frustration and trying to think about what they could do. Bally owned all the rights to Pong, since the game had been submitted as the videogame portion of the contract between the two companies. Even if they decided that they wanted to try to manufacture it themselves, they were legally and ethically proscribed from doing so.

Ted further explains: "That's when I said, 'Either we build it ourselves or we go home. I don't want to go home!' We went over what the costs would be and Nolan and Al agreed that we couldn't afford to do it. I echoed my statement and said that we needed to make a decision. I said, 'If we decide to build it ourselves then we can work on how to get it done. If not, we go home.'"

In the end, none of them opted for going home. Ted said he would handle the TVs and cabinets, and Al and Nolan could work on the boards

puppy pon

Tennis For Two
» YEAR: 1958
» SYSTEM: ANALOGUE COMPUTER/OSCILLOSCOPE

William Higinbotham fiddled around with one of Brookhaven National Laboratory's early computers for calculating missile trajectories to simulate a crude game of tennis. We're betting productivity at Brookhaven dropped dramatically.

Top Players Tennis
» YEAR: 1989
» SYSTEM: NES

This is the earliest example we could find of a celebrity-endorsed tennis game. The players in question are Chris Evert and Ivan Lendl. It also allows four people to play at the same time, as long as you have the relevant NES adaptor.

Super Tennis
» YEAR: 1991
» SYSTEM: SNES

Although it's not the most innovative game in our selection, Super Tennis definitely deserves to be here. It's quite simply the best 16-bit tennis game ever made, with a masterful selection of shots and incredibly nippy gameplay. Nice Mode 7 court effects as well.

Jennifer Capriati Tennis
» YEAR: 1992
» SYSTEM: MEGA DRIVE

There are lots of tennis titles that focus around classic male players, but this is the only one to be based on a popular female tennis star. While it plays a decent game of tennis, there are more notable titles to feature celebrity endorsements.

Pete Sampras Tennis
» YEAR: 1994
» SYSTEM: MEGA DRIVE, GAME GEAR

This fun offering from Codemasters featured Pete Sampras and was the first game to utilize the company's J-Cart technology, allowing two pads to be plugged into the cartridge, and featured some fun mini-games, including a cameo from Dizzy.

ANYONE FOR TENNIS?
A look at the rich and varied world of videogame tennis

Pocket Tennis Color
» YEAR: 1999
» SYSTEM: NEO GEO POCKET

While it lacks the structure of Mario Tennis, this superb little offering remains our favorite handheld tennis game because it's so much fun to play. Sublime controls and an excellent two-player mode make it a timeless portable classic of the genre.

Virtua Tennis 2
» YEAR: 2001
» SYSTEM: ARCADE, DREAMCAST, PS2

Sega's original Virtua Tennis was so good that it became an extremely hard formula for Sega to improve on. It managed it, though, thanks to even more players and an improved single-player campaign, along with a pile of excellent mini-games.

Mario Tennis
» YEAR: 2000
» SYSTEM: NINTENDO 64, GAME BOY COLOR

Camelot's excellent tennis game proved that, with the right care, Mario could work in anything. Mini-games galore, excellent gameplay and a motley crew of Nintendo favorites turned Mario Tennis into one of the N64's best sports games.

Outlaw Tennis
» YEAR: 2005
» SYSTEM: XBOX, PS2

An unusual tennis game, because the only endorsement isn't a player but political satirist Stephen Colbert, who commentates. While it tries to shock with its cast – a PhD stripper, a convict and a Jewish ninja, among others – it plays a rather rudimentary game of tennis.

Wii Sports
» YEAR: 2006
» SYSTEM: WII

The pack-in game for Nintendo's Wii featured a truly wonderful game of tennis that really came into its own thanks to the innovative motion controls. The sequel in Wii Sports Resort was better thanks to MotionPlus control, but the original remains so much fun to play, especially with two players.

» In an effort to expand its locations and potential buyers, Atari promoted Pong to department stores and doctor's offices. Seen here is a flyer for Dr Pong and Puppy Pong, which are simply Pong housed in a waiting-room-friendly cabinet.

and components. Nolan and Ted then crafted a letter to Bally as well as their strategy for when Nolan went in to meet with its management. In a move that would make Obi-Wan Kenobi proud, they convinced Bally that this wasn't the droid it was looking for. An incredible feat, considering that Bally's subsidiary, Midway, was actually interested in releasing the game. Nolan managed to talk them out of it by playing both groups against each other, claiming to each that the other didn't want *Pong* so that in the end, they really didn't. Per Ted's suggestion, they offered to replace it with another game, but only if Bally formally rejected *Pong*, returning the rights to Atari. When the formal letter came, the ruse had worked, but better than they had expected. Bally had canceled the entire contract, including the pinball machine.

Ted set about designing the now-famous bright yellow and woodgrain cabinet and getting the television sets they'd need to modify to put in the cabinets. The plan was to make 50 *Pong* cabinets to sell, a modest amount but one that would still strain the small amount of storage space they had in which to manufacture them.

a problem because of their line of credit through a local bank. Then, suddenly, two weeks later, he received a call that the cabinets were ready, to come pick them up. There was no way Ted or Nolan had the transportation, but Hurlbut delivered them – all 50 at once. Atari didn't have the room for all of them inside the small leased area, let alone room to do the work to install the components.

By chance, though, the candle maker next door happened to move out in the middle of the night, leaving a vacancy. Without asking permission, Ted used a

"Without Pong, you'd have no Coleco or Nintendo entering videogames"

After the design for the cabinet was done, Ted started looking for someone to manufacture them in bulk. After one false start that was too cheaply put together, he found the answer in the form of PS Hurlbut, a local cabinet maker. Ted said they might not be able to pay for them all at once, but the owner said it was not

sabre saw to cut a large hole through the wall separating the two properties. Now they had plenty of room!

Ted also used his own money to pick up 50 13-inch black-and-white Hitachi TV sets that were going to be taken apart and used for the monitors inside each Pong unit. Costing $3,000 in total, the investment out of his own pocket was well worth it in his mind. They had a chance to make more money in the long run.

In the meantime, Nolan had a slightly easier job getting the PCB manufacturing going. He literally just walked across the lot from their rental unit to another one where a small PCB manufacturer was located. Though he and Al also tracked down sources for the rest of the parts they needed, Nolan's overall job was... well, nobody really knew.

It was 27 November, and Ted and Al set about assembling the units, as did a few of the other people they had taken on. But Nolan largely stood around, watching while everyone assembled. Ted walked up to him and said: "What are you doing? We're assembling these things; now it's your job to go sell them."

With what Ted describes as a "hang dog" look, Nolan went back to his office to

PONG MEMORIES

Pong was such a seminal, powerfully influential game that Bill Budge's first Apple II high-res 6502 program was a *Pong* ball bouncing on the screen, and it blew him away. Creating the original *Pong* experience himself seven years after the original appeared was still an event of magnitude.

John Romero, Loot Drop

start making calls. The price had already been decided: $937 per Pong unit. Picked by Ted after he saw the number on the licence plate of a car in the parking lot, it put them in the sub-$1,000 price point they wanted. Nolan returned only an hour later, looking white as a ghost. After making just three calls, he informed them that he had sold 300 units – 50 to one, 100 to another, and 150 to the last. They were in business!

Legacy

While the Magnavox Odyssey and *Computer Space* had been first in the consumer and coin-op industries respectively, it was *Pong* that would really drive the move towards videogames in the public consciousness and jump-start both industries. By June of 1973, Atari had already sold 3,500 units, which was stellar in a time when most runs of traditional coin-op games like pinball were 1,500 units. At the end of its manufacturing life, around 8,000 units were sold. This was all in the midst of an explosion of *Pong* clones by other manufacturers, including Bally/Midway.

PONG

PONG SEQUELS

Pong Doubles (September 1973)
The first follow-up to *Pong*. *Pong Doubles* moves the game into a four-player variant by re-creating the doubles tennis format. Four staggered paddles controlled by four separate spinners create a unique co-operative version of *Pong*.

Super Pong (February 1974)
This adds three paddles to the player's spinner and random starting points for the ball's serve. The three-paddle horizontal format was later leveraged vertically in games like Atari's *Avalanche* and Activision's *Kaboom!*.

Quadrapong (March 1974)
This is another move by *Pong* into the four-player realm. In this version, each player guards their own goal with their individual paddle. The player can only miss four times before their goal closes up and they're out of the game.

Pin Pong (October 1974)
The first pinball videogame, done *Pong*-style. It was still just a ball and paddle, but in this case the flippers were the paddles. There are no real flippers on screen; an image of a paddle angled to the real horizontal one is quickly substituted to create the illusion.

Tournament Table (March 1978)
This is a collection of all of Atari's paddle-and-ball games in a single cocktail-style arcade cabinet. *Breakout*, *Quadrapong*, *Foozpong*, *Handball*, and multiple variants of *Soccer*, *Hockey* and *Basketball*.

PONG MEMORIES

Pong was probably my most desired toy that I never actually got. I loved the game – used to play in arcades – but it was always that little bit too expensive for us to buy. You can imagine my awe when I actually got to meet and subsequently become friends with Nolan Bushnell! Life is funny sometimes.
Gary Bracey, Ocean Software

» The inside of the first Pong. A simple wooden shelf with a standard 13-inch black-and-white Hitachi that Ted picked up. The prototype Pong sits in the bottom of the cabinet.

The press jumped on the new medium, whose name still hadn't been defined yet. It could be regularly seen labeled as TV tennis, TV games, Space Age games, video action games, electronic games, television skill games, video skill games, Space Age pinball and just plain videogames. But Atari's *Pong* and *Pong*-flavoured follow-ups were most assuredly in the front.

Pong reached such iconic status that it has influenced pop culture as well, becoming a recognizable symbol of the Seventies, with appearances in movies and television shows from that decade onward.

The impact of *Pong* on the industry simply cannot be dismissed or diminished. It launched Atari, the company that was then synonymous with videogames and high technology, solidified and trumpeted the home videogame industry, and launched entire genres that branch from it, like the *Breakout/Arkanoid* style of games.

Pong, in all its simplicity, completely revolutionized the way we look at interactive entertainment. It created an acceptance of the amusement industry at a time when it was associated with organized crime and back-room bars, and it showed the promise of the future of high technology as it was just entering the public consciousness.

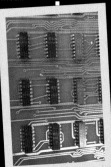

Without the impact of *Pong*, you'd have no companies like Coleco or Nintendo entering videogames, both of which started with clones of the game. It was Atari's Japanese coin-op division, which started out making *Pong* machines in Japan, that was sold to Namco to become its own videogame division. Likewise, jukebox company Konami was inspired to enter the videogame industry after the success of *Pong*. There are also the legions of game programmers, on just about every platform imaginable, who cut their teeth programming versions of *Pong* as their 'Hello world' beginner's app. *Pong* or versions of it have been ported to any system you care to mention precisely because of this, and the principles of the game are still used to this day to teach programming skills.

With its recognition in museums and archives around the globe, *Pong*'s importance to industry and culture has come to its highest level. Without its astonishing popularity, many companies would not have invested time and resources building affordable home consoles. And now, here we are, 46 years later, paying homage to the game that started as a warm-up and truly warmed up the industry. Anyone for tennis?

Even though it would be manufactured in a variety of shapes and sizes, this grinning orange Hoppity Hop is often considered to be the 'original'.

Information

Manufacturer: Ledragomma
First Released: 1969
Expect to pay: $9.99

HOPPITY HOP

They were exhausting, they were chaotic, and they were a lot of fun. Hoppity Hops were the coolest way for kids to get around, bouncing on a giant rubber ball with a grinning monster face painted on the front. Hoppity Hops originated in Italy, where they were created by Aquilino Cosani, inventor of the Swiss ball and co-owner of the firm Ledragomma. He called the toy 'Pon-Pon' when he patented the idea in 1968, but it wasn't long before its popularity saw a host of imitators. Mettoy was the first company to bring Hoppity Hops to the UK market, which were originally a blue color. The revised version, in orange with ribbed handles, would soon follow and become the 'iconic' Hoppity Hop.

Hoppity Hops were designed for children to use, which meant they were the right size for small legs to kick off the ground. It was much harder for adults to use Hoppity Hops, owing to the fact they had much longer legs! Larger 'adult' versions were later made.

Their enduring popularity means Hoppity Hop events are still being held, such as Hoppity Hop races. Ashrita Furman is the fastest man in the world on a Hoppity Hop, doing the 100 meters race in 30.2 seconds.

If you think Ashrita Furman's 100-metre dash record is too hard to beat, his other record is even tougher. He's raced the fastest mile on a Hoppity Hop, covering the distance in 15 minutes and three seconds along the Great Wall of China!

Comp. Retail £11.42	Argos Price £7.95

2. Sunbeam by Raleigh "Chippy" Cycle. With built-in stabilizers. Rear wheel 9" (22.8 cm). For inside leg 14½" to 17½" (36.8 to 44.4 cm)...Cat. No. 350/6491

Comp. Retail £11.45	Argos Price £9.45

3. Tri-ang "Mars" Trike. Adjustable seat. For inside leg 15" to 17" (38.1 to 43.2 cm)......Cat. No. 350/6460

Comp. Retail £11.75	Argos Price £8.95

4. Bantel Racer Trike. Adjustable steel seat. Cat. No. 350/0136

Comp. Retail £7.66	Argos Price £5.25

5. Play-Way "Scorpion" Pavement Cycle. Detachable stabilizers. Front wheel cable brake. 12" (30.5 cm) wheels. For inside leg 13½" to 17" (34.3 to 43.2 cm)........Cat. No. 350/5155

Comp. Retail £25.25	Argos Price £17.45

6. Bantel 3-Wheel Scooter. Height 30" (76.2 cm). Cat. No. 350/0129

Comp. Retail £6.23	Argos Price £4.25

7. "Pony" Pavement Cycle. Detachable stabilizers. Front wheel cable brake. 12" (30.5 cm) wheels. For inside leg 15" to 19" (38.1 to 48.2 cm). Cat. No. 350/6518

Comp. Retail £21.99	Argos Price £17.95

8. Dekkertoys "Olympic" Punchball Mk. II. Mounted on a wooden footboard. Height to centre of ball; adjustable from 36" to 45" (91.4 to 114.3 cm)....................Cat. No. 350/5571

Comp. Retail £7.55	Argos Price £4.99

9. Crescent "Cheyenne" Rifle. 100 shot repeater cap rifle. Length 28" (71.1 cm)...Cat. No. 350/5595

Comp. Retail £2.56	Argos Price £1.75

10. Wembley "Spacehopper". Moulded vinyl. Inflates to 60" (152.4 cm) circ......Cat. No. 350/0026

Comp. Retail £3.03	Argos Price £1.99

11. Dekkertoys Wendy House. Tubular plastic frame. Flame retarded cotton walls with PVC roof and door. Size 46"×30"×46" high to apex (116.8×76.2×116.8 cm)......Cat. No. 350/5588

Comp. Retail £8.55	Argos Price £5.75

12. Flyer Senior Roller Skates. Ball bearing wheels. Adjustable for shoe sizes 9 junior to 8 adult (27 to 42)...................Cat. No. 350/5564

Comp. Retail £6.10	Argos Price £4.25

13. Crescent "Texas" Double Holster Set. 2 die cast metal 100 shot repeater pistols. Length of gun 8¼" (20.9 cm)................Cat. No. 350/5605

Comp. Retail £2.61	Argos Price £1.75

THE LEGACY

Although Hoppity Hops have declined in popularity, one aspect of them stubbornly lives on – world record attempts. In March 2013, the world record was set in Johannesburg for the most people simultaneously hopping for one minute, when 2,943 people beat the previous record of 2,518.

Information

Manufacturer: Hasbro/Milton Bradley
First Released: 1967
Expect to pay: $20-40 CIB unit,
$40-$50 NIB refill packs

Back in 2005, Lite-Brite FX Flash Art catapulted our retro toy's dependable craft concept way outside the proverbial light box. In a kind of 2000s take on spin art, this extreme multimedia unit had kids dripping neon paint onto a constantly spinning, strobing, musical turntable. A strange, arguably non-Lite Brite revision.

Given the toy's main illuminating feature, it's easy to assume how Lite-Brite's rhyming moniker may have originated. Interestingly, inventor Joseph M Burck instead named the glowing art device after Senator J William Fulbright and the Fulbright US Student Programme, which still promotes educational opportunities for recent college graduates all around the world.

In 2010, Texas-based Christian rock group David Crowder Band released a popular music video for their song SMS (Shine) which was filmed almost entirely by way of stop-motion animation. Lite-Brite sequences, forms and animals are seen crossing between the toy light box and the real world, creating some truly captivating peg-centric moments.

According to Guinness World Records, the largest Lite-Brite picture ever created was a mural that used 596,897 individual colored pegs. It was composed by artist Ta-coumba Aiken and illuminated for the first time in Minnesota on 16 February 2013. The piece was emblazoned with the phrase "Forever Saint Paul".

THE LEGACY

Over 50 years after its initial retail debut, Lite-Brite is still glowing strong. Multiple decades have seen various product refreshments, like a four-sided cube for quadruple the creations, a Glow Art black light set that solely utilized fluorescent markers, the micro "World's Smallest" Lite-Brite and a tablet-style redesign that integrated portability, reusable overlays and more user-friendly molded pegs. Lite-Brite also entered the digital age back in 2010 with an official iPad/iPhone app that allowed users to compose screen-bound works of art.

LITE-BRITE

"Lite-Brite, making things with light, out of sight, making things with Lite-Brite!"

LEDs are currently all the rage, but back in the 1970s, creative kids were getting an electronic jump on today's futuristic illumination. A sort of ingenious primitive precursor to many modern backlit devices, Lite-Brite was originally created by toy designer Joseph M Burck and subsequently farmed out to Hasbro for mass production. The crafty gadget's premise was deceptively simple: a single bulb shone through a boxed grid, which was then adorned with various black paper overlays for artistic guidance. Multi-colored plastic pegs could then be pushed through the printed patterns, creating all manner of brilliant, glowing, light box masterpieces.

Available templates over the years included a huge assortment of licensed properties, including the likes of Scooby-Doo, GI Joe, Mickey Mouse, The Muppets, Ghostbusters, Gremlins, My Little Pony, Fraggle Rock, Talespin, Transformers and even a ridiculous Mr T refill pack. Still, if authoritative instructions were too much of a restraint, you could always go rogue and devise your own rainbow Mona Lisa via blank sheets. With eight different colors of pegs to choose from and plenty of imagination, the possibilities for interesting compositions were virtually endless. Which is a good thing, because the black paper patterns weren't exactly reusable – once they were punctured, it was impossible to remember where each specific peg went.

Lite-Brite's rudimentary proto-tech magic remains a shining beacon of simplicity and ingenuity, reminding current toy makers that fun can be as easy as rearranging hues on a glowing box, even if half the pegs do eventually end up inside the vacuum cleaner.

Information

Manufacturer: Raleigh Bicycle Company
First Released: 1969
Expect to pay: $500

CHOPP

RALEIGH CHOPPER

A rough rider with a smooth look, the Chopper brought cool cycling chic to surburbia

How it began

There is some debate over who actually designed the Raleigh Chopper but one thing's for certain, the bicycle was a true icon of the 1970s. Not only did it catch many an eye with its huge cow horn handle bars, elongated padded seat and back rest, it moved away from the diamond-shaped frames of old while opting for a back wheel significantly larger than the front.

As such, it was a bike that kids would drool over and they'd slap it high on their lists to Santa, despite the first editions costing a whopping $35 (equivalent to $500 today). In many ways, the steep price further enhanced the bike's attraction by giving it increased desirability in the playground. Suddenly the humble bike had transformed from a speedy mode of transport into an achingly cool fashion accessory.

But then it was always meant to be that way. The Chopper was inspired by the dragster motorbikes of the 1960s – the type that looked so good being ridden by Dennis Hopper and Peter Fonda in the counterculture movie Easy Rider. The bicycles had a unique car-like multiple-speed gear stick on the main frame and it was nothing short of a revolution in a country where bike design had tended to be traditional and conservative. The bikes brought a flashy Hells Angels vibe to the back streets of Britain and the United States, but quite how they got there, depends on which story you believe.

The traditional tale has Alan Oakley, the head of Raleigh's design department, sketching the bike on the back of an airmail envelope on a return flight from America, a country he visited to get a better handle on youth culture (he claims to have seen Californian teenagers customizing their bicycles to look like dragster motorbikes).

This has long been contested by Tom Karen, former managing director of the consultancy firm Ogle Design which was used by Raleigh. Karen says he was tasked with coming up with the designs in a bid to rival Schwinn's similarly ape-handled Sting-Ray.

Either way, the effect was the same and a cult classic was born. The first prototypes were tested in 1968 and the debut version was released in the United States the following year, complete with a choice of three- and five-speed Sturmey Archer gear hubs and high back rests. These failed to sell in huge quantities but Raleigh was undeterred. It launched the MK1, bringing it to the UK, and kids immediately went crazy over them.

Going global

The Easy Rider film and its customized Harley-Davidsons (named Captain America and Billy Bike) had helped matters no end. While most kids wouldn't have seen the X-rated movie, many parents had became familiar with its carefully cultivated image and the presence of those custom motorcycles helped make the outrageous Chopper design more acceptable to those with the buying power (it's a fair bet that many parents secretly wanted one for themselves).

It didn't seem to matter that the ride itself wasn't the smoothest, nor that the steering was difficult. Kids also seemed to get over the fact that the high center of gravity made hilly journeys a struggle. That's because the Mark 1 really was all about the design: the 20-inch rear wheel four inches larger than the front, the wide chunky treaded tires, the seat that had riders sitting far back over the rear wheel, and a kickstand that allowed the cycle to lean like a parked motorbike.

"The Raleigh Chopper bikes brought a flashy Hells Angels vibe to the back streets of Britain but quite how they got there, depends on which story you believe"

To that end, Raleigh was already riding on a high and the company was knocking them out in droves at its factory in Nottingham where each bike was made by hand. But it was also attracting negative attention over its safety record not only in the US but the UK too.

The issue was raised in the House of Commons by Labor MP Phillip Whitehead who called on the Secretary of State for the Environment to consider "prohibiting the manufacture of Chopper-style high handlebar bicycles for children". He said an article in the British Medical Journal suggested there was an accident rate of 69 percent for such bikes, despite them making up just 20 percent of the total.

There were also warnings about double-riding and concerns that the bikes would wobble at speed. It prompted a redesign from 1972, adding a five-speed derailleur option (that very few bought) and a modified gear handle that sat between the legs and added a sense of maturity. The seat became shorter (albeit still long enough for two) and the handlebars were welded to prevent the bars from being inclined backwards, affecting the steering. A Chopper Sprint was also released, complete with drop handlebars (it was scrapped a year later). "Only the originators, Raleigh Industries of England, could improve such an outstanding innovation," the Mark 2 advert claimed.

Over the course of the 1970s, 1.5 million Choppers were sold in the UK alone and they could be bought in a variety of colors including fizzy lemon, infra red and ultra violet. But even though the Chopper had transformed Raleigh's fortunes and sold in huge numbers across the world (the US had a ban on tall sissy bars but also a very wide spectrum of models and colors), by 1980 it had ceased production. Many desired the Raleigh Grifter which, manufactured from 1976, looked like it had an upside down Chopper frame and came with a three-speed hub and mudguards. The BMX craze also began to take hold.

MOST DESIRABLE!

Mk1 10-speed Chopper

The rarest of all Choppers is a 10-speed Mk1 version made by Raleigh for the American market in 1970 and 1971. It was available in any color as long as it was orange – specifically Bright Orange in 1970 and Pumpkin Orange the following year – but very few people actually bought one, which has upped the scarcity value somewhat.

As such, you'd have to part with about $2,000 to snap one up in great condition, with the models from 1970 proving to be that bit more valuable. They had all of the riding problems associated with those early versions but we'd hazard a guess that you wouldn't want to be sitting on this rare beauty anyway.

Collector's guide

Even so, the Chopper retained its appeal and it would emerge in popular culture from time to time, such as in the pop video for Supergrass' *Alright* in 1995. It was also brought back to life in 2004 as a limited edition Mk3, which remained in production for five years.

Costing between $200 and $300, it came complete with a new seat better made for one rider and there was a gear lever on the handlebars rather than in a groin-threatening position on the frame. It also used aluminium alloy tubing rather than heavy steel. Other models have since been released including one produced for Halfords in 2014 and another in a "scooter cream" coloring in 2016. But the original 1970s models are the ones that are proving most attractive today.

Fuelled by nostalgia, thousands of collectors and enthusiasts invest great sums in their bikes, buying spares and memorabilia on the internet. They have also gathered in Northampton in years gone by for hugely popular events staged by the Raleigh Chopper Owners Club, attended by as many as 3,000.

Decent, well-maintained bikes can sell for in excess of $500 today with new, boxed Mk1 models costing many thousands for those lucky enough to find them. As with any collectibles, scarcity makes the heart grow fonder which is why bagging one of the few steel-wheeled silver jubilee specials from 1976 are still the most sought after.

That said, any Chopper for someone of a certain age is going to draw mist over the eyes. They were, after all, part of an exciting new wave of bicycles and they had bags of personality. Sure, they were unreliable and provided a harsh ride, but the scrapes kids would get into when riding or piggy-backing on them will always live fresh in the mind (and perhaps as scars on the legs). If you could bottle childhood chic, then you would have it right there.

ESSENTIAL MERCH!

Chopper Sprint

Bike dealers wanted a more traditional-looking version of the Chopper to satisfy their conservative buyers so Raleigh came up with the Sprint, replacing the drop handlebars of the original with those more in keeping with a racing bike. Unfortunately, the design was far from innovative and it bombed, but collectors still like to snap them up today.

Gold-plated Chopper

A gold-plated version of the iconic bike was developed in 1976 to mark the production of the millionth Chopper. It had followed on from a Chopper SE which celebrated the 750,000th bike, but other than the coloring the gold version didn't add anything new to the Mk2 model.

Silver Jubilee Model

This Chopper was created as a one-off to commemorate the Queen's Silver Jubilee in 1977 but it was released in August 1976 in the hope of picking up the all-important Christmas sales. It didn't sell in great numbers but looked rather snazzy, both elements combining to make it appealing to collectors.

The game came with two trays, one blue and the other red. Within each of these sat a set of plastic flippers into which the game's 24 face cards would be inserted. Players would pick a character from another set of cards and place it into a slot at the front of the tray. It was then game on!

Joe Charles Eric David Alfred Bill Frans

Sam Alex Paul Peter Philip George

Richard Max Robert Anne Maria Anita

THE LEGACY

There have been many variations since, some replacing the traditional faces with Disney or Marvel characters, for instance, and redesigns to reflect greater diversity. At the same time, some fans have created their own versions, such as one using the faces of US presidents than can be downloaded online and printed. There have been live-action versions, too: mentalist Derren Brown uses it in one of his routines.

According to the instructions, you could not ask whether the person was a man or a woman as your first question. Presumably this was to prevent players quickly narrowing the field if the mystery person was a woman. This was odd because asking if the character was bald or wore a hat with glasses could also get you down to just five possibilities.

GUESS WHO?

Some were bald, some wore hats, some had glasses and some bore the most outrageous of mustaches. But of the 24 faces on an original Guess Who? board, there were just five women and one from an ethnic minority group. True diversity, it has to be said, was not its strongest point back then.

It was, however, a product of its time: a guessing game created by Ora and Theo Coster that had each player picking a card and the other trying to work out whose face may be in it by asking a series of Yes and No questions.

Luck could play a big part and have the game won in no time. "Are they wearing a hat?" answered in the affirmative would see everyone bar Eric, George, Maria, Bernard and Claire instantly eliminated – the face cards satisfyingly flipped down in a clap of plastic-on-plastic. A few more clever questions and you could soon have a winner.

Despite that, Guess Who? was great fun and a real success for Milton Bradley. Key to this was the game's competitive nature since both players were trying to guess their opponent's character at the same time and the victor would be the one who figured it out first (saying, dramatically, "The Mystery Person is...").

There was also a harsh penalty if your opponent guessed incorrectly: they'd automatically lose. That would leave one of you as forlorn-looking as George and the other as smug as smirking Max. Guess who you'd want to be.

You'd keep score by placing one of the supplied pegs into holes positioned towards the front left of each of the plastic boards. The overall champion needed to win five individual games, which meant that a session could take around 20 minutes or so to complete.

The main differences between the faces centered on the size of their noses, the presence of hats and spectacles, the different colored hair (or none at all), styles of mustache and the colors of eyes, cheeks, lips, hats and spectacles. But there were also more subtle differences that could ease you to a victory.

Information

Manufacturer: Milton Bradley
First Released: 1979
Expect to pay: $3

70 FILMS THAT DEFINED THE '70s

Your guide to the classics that shaped a generation of cinemagoers

The Seventies were a fantastic decade for movies. There was far more interest in cinema than in the previous decade, which was plain to see by simply looking back at box office reports of the time.

During the Sixties the top ten movies of the decade generated over $1 billion at the box office, an insane number until you realize that the top ten big earners of the Seventies generated closer to $2 billion. That success is largely down to just two films, Jaws and Star Wars, which between them earned over half a billion at the box office and led to what's now known as the summer blockbuster movie.

Several prominent directors also rose to power during the Seventies, including Stephen Spielberg, Francis Ford Coppola, George Lucas, Woody Allen, Martin Scorsese and Stanley Kubrick, all of whom released films that influenced numerous genres in the decades to come. Stars like Clint Eastwood, Richard Gere, John Travolta, Meryl Streep, Robert De Niro and numerous others helped draw in big crowds, while various genres began to receive a rise in popularity, particularly disaster, gangster and horror movies. With that in mind we've curated 70 of the best films of the 70s.

Some are stone cold classics; some were box office bombs that slowly grew into cult classic status, others are simply personal favorites. How many have you seen?

© IMPAwards.com

27

Love Story

1970

1 This tragic romantic drama was adapted by author Erich Segal from his best-selling novel. It helped establish leads, Ryan O'Neal and Ali Macgraw as huge stars and it became a smash hit at the box office with a domestic gross of over $136 million. A sequel, *Oliver's Story*, was released in 1978 to far lesser acclaim.

Airport

1970

2 This epic drama populated the disaster movies that became rife during the Seventies. Burt Lancaster and Dean Martin lead a solid ensemble cast with Lancaster excelling as the airport manager who has to deal with the mother of all snowstorms and a suicide bomber. Punters loved the drama and it netted over $100 million at the box office.

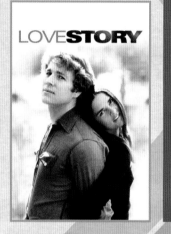

M*A*S*H ▲

1970

3 After over a dozen directors passed it over, director Robert Altman steered an adaptation of a little known Korean War-era novel to box office gold. The rich ensemble cast (something Altman would excel at with later movies) includes the likes of Donald Sutherland, Elliott Gould, Tom Skerritt and Sally Kellerman, and became such a success that it spawned a hit TV series.

Patton

1970

4 *Patton* won big at the Academy Awards scooping seven Oscars, including Best Picture, Best Director and Best Original Screenplay. Arguably the most deserved award went to George C Scott who gives a phenomenal performance as the famous senior US officer. A sequel, *The Last Days Of Patton*, once again starred Scott and was released in 1986.

Gimme Shelter

1970

5 It took three directors to film this influential documentary that focuses on the Rolling Stones as they finish the final weeks of their US tour and take part in the infamous Altamont Free Concert. It features some astonishing behind the scenes footage, including the fatal stabbing of 18-year-old African-American Meredith Hunter.

The Last Picture Show

1971

6 Peter Bogdanovich's epic coming of age movie stood apart from many of its peers due to the director's decision to shoot in black and white. Despite being nominated for eight Academy Awards, it ended up winning two for the performances of Ben Johnson and Cloris Leachman (who were both up against fellow *The Last Picture Show* actors, Jeff Bridges and Ellen Burstyn).

Fiddler On The Roof

1971

7 Norman Jewison's popular musical scored big at the US box office, securing United Artists's second number one of the decade and over $80 million in the process. It had an equally strong showing at the Oscars, winning three Academy Awards, including Best Music and Original Song Score for composer John Williams.

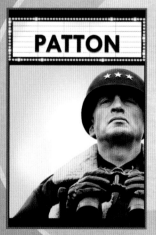

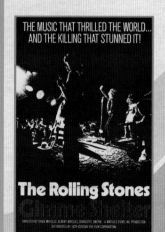

Diamonds Are Forever

1971

9 Moviegoers turned out in their droves to see Sean Connery's last performance as James Bond. They weren't disappointed thanks to a chilling performance from Charles Gray as Bond's nemesis, Ernst Stavro Blofeld and action-packed set pieces. It went on to make over $43 million at the box office. As for Connery he would return as Bond in 1983's *Never Say Never Again.*

Escape From The Planet Of The Apes

1971

12 This enthralling sci-fi movie is generally considered to be the best of the four sequels that followed in the wake of *Planet Of The Apes.* Roddy McDowall returns as Cornelius and finds himself stuck on 1973 Earth after going through a time warp. It ended up making six times its original $2-million budget and was followed by *Conquest Of The Planet Of The Apes* the following year.

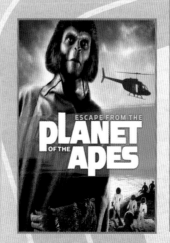

Dirty Harry

1971

10 Clint Eastwood's hard-hitting portrayal of Inspector "Dirty" Harry Callahan helped cement him as one of the big action stars of the Seventies and did big business at the box office earning nearly $36 million off a $4-million budget. It was followed by four sequels, with the last, *The Dead Pool,* released in 1988.

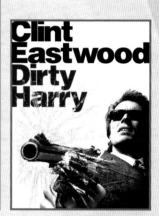

A Clockwork Orange

1971

13 Stanley's Kubrick's brilliant adaptation of Anthony Burgess' cult dystopian novel caused such controversy on its release that the film was subsequently pulled in Britain in 1973 at the request of Kubrick himself. It wasn't until after Kubrick died in 1999 that the film was eventually re-released in cinemas and in the home market, allowing viewers to finally legally view his astonishingly dark masterpiece.

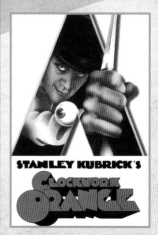

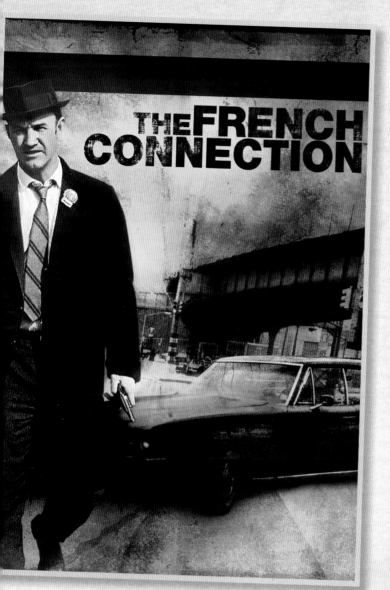

The French Connection ▲

1971

8 William Friedkin's adaptation of Robin Moore's popular novel is notable for being the first R-rated movie to win Best Picture at the Academy Awards. The tight, tensely-paced thriller would score four additional awards, including ones for Friedkin and Gene Hackman, who delivers a powerful performance as Det. Jimmy 'Popeye' Doyle. Hackman would return for a sequel in 1975.

Willy Wonka And The Chocolate Factory

1971

11 While it was a box office disaster (it just managed to make back its $3-million budget) Mel Stuart's delightful movie started rising in popularity during the Eighties and is now considered a true classic. It works thanks to fantastic performances from its young child cast and the genius casting of Gene Wilder as the whimsical Willy Wonka.

Get Carter

1971

14 Michael Caine is superb as the London gangster who heads to Newcastle to investigate the accidental death of his brother. Famed for its gritty and realistic portrayal of criminal behavior and excessive violence, it has influenced directors such as Guy Ritchie and has an appalling remake, which starred the gruff Sylvester Stallone.

Shaft

1971

15 Gordon Parks' Shaft was one of the first major Blaxploitation movies and set a template for both its sequels and copycat clones. It is well known for its killer soundtrack composed by Isaac Hayes as well as a blistering performance from Richard Roundtree as the titular hero. It's also featured in dozens of pop culture references. A fourth film, starring Samuel L Jackson as Shaft's nephew, was released in 2002.

Klute ▼

1971

16 Jane Fonda rightfully won an Oscar for her stunning performance as a high-priced prostitute who assists Donald Sutherland's detective in a missing person case. While the story itself isn't the most gripping, it's elevated by both Fonda and Sutherland's stunning performances, which really turn it into something unmissable. It would go on to be considered the first part of Alan J Pakula's "paranoia trilogy" alongside The Parallax View and All The President's Men.

The Godfather

1972

17 Francis Ford Coppola's deft direction of Mario Puzo's best-selling novel is widely considered to be one of the greatest gangster movies of all time. Filled with exceptional performances and led by Marlon Brando, it features an incredible turn by Al Pacino and became Paramount's most successful movie at that time, taking over $133 million from a $6-million budget.

The Poseidon Adventure

1972

18 20th Century Fox's epic disaster movie was far more buoyant than the ship it took place on thanks to five Oscar winners in the cast, including Gene Hackman, Shelley Winters and Ernest Borgnine. Expertly paced and with drama and danger around every corner, it's filled with spectacular effects (it would win Best Visual Effects in 1972) and spawned a disastrous sequel, *Beyond The Poseidon Adventure*, in 1979.

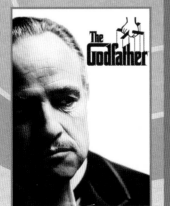

What's Up, Doc? ▶

1972

19 This screwball comedy riffed off the popular comedy movies of the 1930s and the cartoons of Bugs Bunny. The end result is a zany comedy that focuses on the owners of four plaid bags (it's a lot funnier than it sounds) and proves to be a fun homage to classics such as *Bringing Up Baby*. Audiences agreed and it made $66 million off a lowly $4-million budget.

Deliverance

1972

20 You'll never listen to a banjo the same way again after experiencing John Boorman's tense thriller. Notorious for its infamous male rape scene and the fact that the production wasn't insured (meaning every actor had to do their own stunts), *Deliverance* is a taut, jangling thriller that features superb performances from Jon Voight, Ned Beatty and Burt Reynolds as the city boys who fall foul of the Georgia locals.

Cabaret

1972

21 Despite its links to numerous controversies, including Nazism and sexual ambiguity, Bob Fosse's loose adaptation of the 1966 Broadway musical did big business for Allied Artists. It also earned Liza Minnelli her sole Oscar and turned her into a gay icon. *Cabaret* ended up winning eight awards and redeemed Fosse after his box office failure, *Sweet Charity*.

The Getaway

1972

22 This high stakes crime caper received middling reviews on release, which just shows how wrong some critics can be. Directed by Sam Peckinpah, it features Steve McQueen in a typically cool role as a mastermind robber and the then in demand Ali MacGraw as his partner in crime. Stylishly cool and with some intense violence, a disappointing remake appeared in 1994 as a vehicle for Alex Baldwin and Kim Basinger.

The Exorcist

1973

23 This terrifying movie was effectively, though unofficially, banned in the UK for years, only being made available again after it was re-released in 1998. It's a terrifying movie, largely thanks to an astonishingly creepy performance from Linda Blair as a possessed child. Claimed to be cursed and with numerous directors turning it down, it was down to William Friedkin and William Peter Blatty (the original novelist) to steer the film to international success.

Enter The Dragon

1973

25 Many consider Bruce Lee's fifth and final full movie to be the greatest martial arts film of all time and it's difficult to argue otherwise. While the story is fairly throwaway, it works thanks to its exhilarating fight scenes and a truly mesmerizing performance from Lee. Hugely influential and endlessly parodied it's a painful reminder of just how big an action star Lee could have become.

THE STING

The Sting

1973

24 Paul Newman and Robert Redford's second onscreen pairing delighted both audiences and critics. It powered to the number one position with over $156 million and won seven of its ten Oscar nominations. Interestingly, its producer, the late Julia Phillips, became the first ever woman to win an Oscar as a producer. She would later oversee both *Taxi Driver* and *Close Encounters Of The Third Kind*.

> **"It became so popular that Moore would go on to star in six more Bond movies"**

American Graffiti

`1973`

27 Before he reinvented cinema with *Star Wars*, George Lucas made this delightful slice of small-time Americana for a staggeringly modest $770,000. Basing the film on his own teenage experiences, Lucas assembled a strong ensemble cast that included the likes of Richard Dreyfuss and Ron Howard and an equally impressive soundtrack that ended up going triple platinum. It's memorable for marking the first onscreen appearance of a certain Harrison Ford.

Mean Streets

`1973`

28 While it wasn't his first movie, *Mean Streets* arguably became the first Martin Scorsese movie, focusing on the numerous themes that would highlight much of his later, much more refined, work. It's also notable for being the first of nine films that Scorsese made with Robert De Niro, who somehow manages to upstage the always watchable and equally intense Harvey Keitel.

Westworld

`1973`

29 In many ways, Westworld is effectively a dry run for Michael Crichton's later novel/film one-two, *Jurassic Park*. Crichton's directorial debut features similar themes and looks at what happens when man attempts to create things and how he inevitably loses control in the process. A sequel, *Futureworld*, arrived in 1976, with a short-running TV series, *Beyond Westworld*, appearing in 1980. HBO successfully rebooted the franchise for TV in 2016.

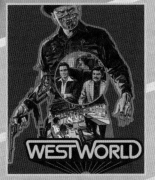

The Wicker Man

`1973`

30 *The Wicker Man*'s horrific ending lingers long in the memory, marking it as one of the great British horror films of the era. It helps that the cast is resoundingly solid too, with Edward Woodward on particularly fine form as the earnest Sergeant who quickly realizes he's painfully and dangerously out of his depth. The 2006 remake starring Nicholas Cage is also horrific, but for completely different reasons.

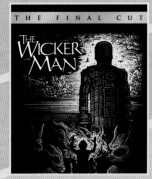

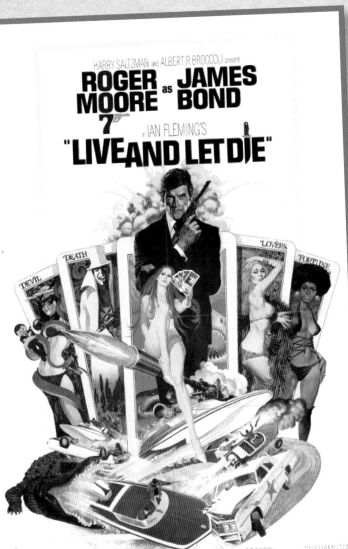

Live And Let Die ▲

`1973`

26 The eighth Bond film marked a number of firsts for the franchise. It was the first to feature new Bond, Roger Moore (who was a sprightly 45 when he took on the role), had the most successful Bond theme and is the first Bond film to feature a romantic relationship with an African-American Bond girl. It became so popular that Moore would go on to star in six more Bond movies throughout the Seventies and early Eighties.

ONE TINY SPARK BECOMES A NIGHT OF BLAZING SUSPENSE

The Fire Chief
STEVE McQUEEN

The Architect
PAUL NEWMAN

WILLIAM HOLDEN

FAYE DUNAWAY

20th CENTURY-FOX and WARNER BROS. present

IRWIN ALLEN'S production of

THE TOWERING INFERNO

Don't Look Now

1973

31 This highly influential horror thriller from Nicolas Roeg is notorious for a controversial sex scene that led many to believe its two stars (Donald Sutherland and Julie Christie) had unsimulated sex. Graphic sex scene aside, *Don't Look Now* is a masterfully directed film that is steeped in thematic motifs and deftly mixes the thriller genre with occult horror. Highly impactful, it's influenced a host of film makers, from Danny Boyle to Lynne Ramsey.

Blazing Saddles

1974

32 *Blazing Saddles* went on to become 1974's year's highest-grossing movie. Deliberately anachronistic, some of its comedy certainly cuts close to the bone due to its political incorrectness but there's no denying that scenes like the campfire and pie fight will have you crying with laughter.

▲ The Towering Inferno

1974

3 3 This award-winning disaster movie marked the first time in Hollywood history that two separate companies (Warner Bros and 20th Century Fox) teamed up to co-produce a film. Like the best disaster movies it's fraught with danger, has tantalizing set pieces and an epic ensemble cast led by Hollywood hardmen, Steve McQueen and Paul Newman. Interestingly, it's based on two separate novels, *The Tower* and *The Glass Inferno*.

Young Frankenstein

1974

34 Not content with busting audiences' guts with *Blazing Saddles*, Mel Brooks also released his hilarious parody of classic horror films in the same year. Once again teaming up with Gene Wilder (who wrote the screenplay alongside Brooks) it was boldly shot in black and white and is littered with classic scenes and hilarious one-liners.

The Godfather Part 2

1974

35 Many feel that Francis Ford Coppola's sequel manages to improve on his original masterpiece. In addition to focusing on Al Pacino's Michael Corleone, it also continually cuts to a separate story revealing how his farther Vito (played by Robert De Niro) rose to power. It's arguably every bit as good as the original thanks to a strong ensemble cast and Coppola's obsession with authenticity. A final chapter arrived in 1990.

Chinatown

1974

36 Robert Towne's delightfully convoluted tale won him Best Original Screenplay at the Academy Awards. It's acclaimed for its multi-layered story, heavy leaning on classic film noir and sterling performances from leads, Jack Nicholson and Faye Dunaway. It also earned director, Roman Polanski a Best Director nomination and received a sequel in 1990 called The Two Jakes, with Jack Nicholson taking over directorial duties.

Texas Chainsaw Massacre

1974

37 Tobe Hooper's video nasty was cheekily sold to punters as a true story, when it was in fact completely made up. Hooper took inspiration from murderer Ed Gein while creating his iconic killer, Leatherface, but that's where the reality ends. Incredibly gory and banned in several countries, including the UK, it's now considered to be one of the greatest horror films of all time and has had several sequels, as well as a remake in 2006.

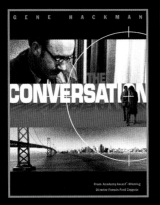

The Conversation

1974

38 1974 was as incredibly prolific year for Francis Ford Coppola, and saw him releasing three films, two of which earned him critical acclaim. Influenced by Michelangelo Antonioni's *Blowup*, *The Conversation* asks audiences what they would do if they inadvertently became privy to a murder. It's an intriguing premise that works brilliantly thanks to Gene Hackman's deep performance as a surveillance expert who unwittingly uncovers the murder in question.

Jaws

1975

39 Fraught with difficulties due to its lengthy sea shoot, Stephen Spielberg's adaptation of Peter Benchley's novel is widely considered to be (along with *Star Wars*) the first summer blockbuster. Its deft combination of solid character acting, dramatic action scenes, wondrous score, high concept premise and aggressive advertising led to it becoming the highest-grossing film of all time (at least until *Star Wars* came along) making $260 million off a $9-million budget. Just try to ignore the largely disappointing sequels, just as Spielberg did.

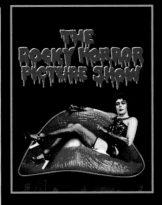

The Rocky Horror Picture Show

1975

40 Richard O'Brien's smash hit musical was such a success it was soon made into a movie. Jim Sharman took on directorial duties, with O'Brien helping him to adapt the screenplay. Many of the original stage actors, including O'Brien and Tim Curry resumed their original roles, with Susan Sarandon and Barry Bostwick being drafted in to add a little star status. The result was a worldwide hit that raked in nearly $139 million. Only Spielberg's *Jaws* was able to best it.

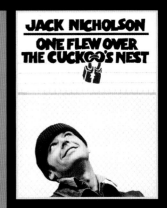

One Flew Over The Cuckoo's Nest

1975

41 Originally starting off life as a Broadway show, its star, Kirk Douglas was keen to turn *One Flew Over The Cuckoo's Nest* into a movie. No one in Hollywood was interested however, so Douglas passed the rights over to his son, Michael, who was able to broker a deal. Danny DeVito resumed his role of Martini, with Jack Nicholson taking on lead duties due to Douglas Snr being considered too old. The change proved a canny one, earning the film five Oscars, including the first of three Best Actor wins for Nicholson.

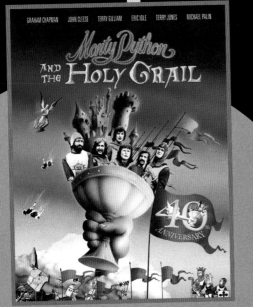

▲ Monty Python And The Holy Grail

1975

42 The first proper movie from the Python team remains absolutely hilarious to watch, filled with killer jokes and hilarious funny set pieces. Effectively spoofing the Arthurian legend, it highlighted the many strengths of the Pythons and helped launch a successful career for co-director, Terry Gilliam. It would form the basis of Eric Idle's *Spamalot* some 30 years later.

Rocky

1976

43 In addition to taking on the lead role, Sylvester Stallone also wrote the screenplay of *Rocky*, the film that helped turn him into an international superstar. Filled with excellent choreography and iconic scenes (everyone remembers those steps) it became a huge box office success and led to seven sequels, with the latest, *Creed III*, being released this year (2023).

A Star Is Born

1976

44 This starring vehicle for Barbra Streisand was actually a remake of a remake (the original film was released in 1937, with a follow-up remake starring Judy Garland in 1954). It didn't seem to bother moviegoers however who fell in love with the tale of Streisand's bar singer falling for Kris Kristofferson's destructive famous rock star. It was remade again in 2018 with Lady Gaga and Bradley Cooper, which also became an international success.

◄ All The President's Men

1976

45 The third part of Alan J Pakula's "paranoia trilogy" is a politically charged thriller based on the then recent Watergate Scandal. Robert Redford and Dustin Hoffman are sensational as the two investigative journalists who uncover the shocking events and are ably supported by a sensational supporting cast. Audiences agreed and it became the fourth highest-grossing film of the year.

The Omen

1976

46 Twentieth Century Fox's creepy horror featured decapitations, hangings and other unsettling deaths as an American diplomat (played by Gregory Peck) slowly realizes that his adopted child (a truly chilling Harvey Spencer Stephens) is the Antichrist. Its success spawned numerous sequels, including a reboot in 2006, as well as a 2015 TV series, *Damien*, which lasted for one season.

◄ Taxi Driver

1976

47 Martin Scorsese's hard-hitting thriller features Robert De Niro, Cybill Shepherd and Jodie Foster, with the latter earning her first Academy Award nomination as Iris, a 12-year-old prostitute. Filled with disturbing themes and hard-hitting violence, it became linked to John Hinckley Jr, who attempted to assassinate President Ronald Reagan in order to impress Foster.

35

Carrie

1976

48 *Carrie* is not only notable for acting as a springboard for many young actors, including John Travolta, Amy Irving and Nancy Allen, but also for being one of those rare things – a good Stephen King adaptation, not to mention its often copied ending. Director, Brian De Palma does great work with the adaptation but it's Sissy Spacek as Carrie and Piper Laurie as her terrifying mother who leave the biggest impression.

Close Encounters Of The Third Kind

1977

51 Steven Spielberg followed up *Jaws* with another huge box office smash, this time focusing on extra-terrestrials instead of killer sharks. It's a brilliantly crafted film and features a superb performance from Richard Dreyfuss as the Indianan electrical worker whose life is changed forever after his close encounter. Spielberg eventually released a Director's Cut in 1979 after being unhappy with the original theatrical release. Make sure you watch that version instead.

Star Wars

1977

49 After failing to secure the rights to *Flash Gordon*, director George Lucas decided to create his own space opera. The result not only changed cinema, but became a cultural phenomenon as well and the highest-grossing film of all time (until the release of *E.T. The Extra-Terrestrial* in 1982). Alongside *Jaws*, its spectacular special effects and epic action sequences helped invent the summer blockbuster and it turned Harrison Ford into an international star. Countless sequels have followed, with the most recent, *Star Wars: The Rise of Skywalker*, released in 2019.

Saturday Night Fever

1977

52 No one was as cool as John Travolta during the Seventies. Not content with starring in the popular TV show *Welcome Back, Kotter* and releasing a top ten single, Travolta turned to the silver screen, playing the outrageously cool Tony Manero. Its key dance sequence has been endlessly parodied over the years, while its soundtrack remains the best selling of all time with over 45 million copies sold.

Smokey And The Bandit

1977

50 Burt Reynolds had a number of notable hits during the Seventies but he's perhaps best remembered as Bo "Bandit" Darville. Planned as a low-budget B movie it soon caught the attention of Reynolds whose star power led to interest from Universal Pictures and a deal with Pontiac to effectively launch its new Trans Am. Staggeringly successful (only Star Wars made more money that year) it was succeeded by two sequels, a spin-off and numerous TV movies.

A Bridge Too Far ▲

1977

53 Few war films are as star-studded as Richard Attenborough's 1977 classic, which featured the likes of Anthony Hopkins, Michael Caine, Sean Connery, Robert Redford, James Caan and Dirk Bogarde. Painfully accurate in its depiction of the unsuccessful Operation Market Garden (something that put many American critics off), its main cast all agreed to take substantial pay cuts in order to keep costs down.

The Rescuers

1977

54 Disney's smash hit has been reissued countless times over the last four decades, raking in nearly $170 million for Disney. It's a solid yarn from the House of Mouse thanks to lovable protagonists, an adorable kid and a creepy villain in the form of Geraldine Page's Madame Medusa. It's also the first Disney cartoon to receive a sequel.

Suspiria

1977

55 Dario Argento's supernatural horror remains as terrifying today as it did in 1977. Beautifully shot and with a fantastic score by prog-rock band Goblin, it has influenced numerous horror movies and is rightly considered a cult classic. There was a remake in 2018 by Luca Guadagnino, which featured *Suspiria*'s original star, Jessica Harper, in a smaller role.

Grease

1978

56 Randal Kleiser's adaptation of the 1971 hit musical was a gigantic success, topping the charts to the tune of nearly $160 million. It cemented John Travolta as a superstar, catapulted Olivia Newton John into the limelight and spawned a best-selling soundtrack. An incredibly weak sequel starring Michelle Pfeiffer and Maxwell Caulfield arrived in 1982.

Animal House

1978

57 Before he terrified audiences with *An American Werewolf In London*, John Landis became king of the gross-out movie, creating a template that would influence everything from *Porky's* to *American Pie*. It was not only the first major role for the late John Belushi and grossed over $141 million at the box office, but also the first *National Lampoon* movie to get a theatrical release.

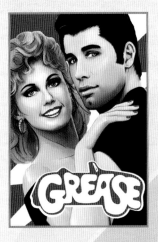

The Deer Hunter

1978

59 Michael Cimino's sensational war drama may run for three hours but you'd never guess it. It's a brilliantly edited piece of work full of deep motives and themes, a gorgeous soundtrack and countless iconic moments, including that infamous Russian roulette scene. Critically acclaimed, it won five Academy Awards and earned Streep her first of 21 Oscar nominations, a record no one has ever equaled.

Every Which Way But Loose

1978

58 It's a brave actor that plays second fiddle to an ape but that's exactly what Clint Eastwood did in James Fargo's action comedy. Despite being warned not to take the role, Eastwood excels as the trucker who tours the country with his pet orangutan, Clive. A sequel, *Any Which Way You Can*, arrived in 1980.

Halloween

`1978`

60 John Carpenter's slasher movie spawned countless imitators and cemented Jamie Lee Curtis (in her debut role) as one of the biggest "Scream Queens" of modern cinema. Made for just $300,000, *Halloween*'s $70 million in takings gave Carpenter huge creative freedom for later films and led to seven sequels, including a remake of the first two movies by the one and only Rob Zombiein 2007. In 2018, a direct sequel to the original film was released and directed by David Gordon Green. It was followed by *Halloween Kills* in 2021 and *Halloween Ends* in 2022, all featuring Jamie Lee Curtis as lead role.

Days Of Heaven

`1978`

61 Terrence Malick's gorgeous-looking film was a box office disaster that even Richard Gere couldn't save, with the film barely clawing back its $3-million budget. Silly audiences missed out though, as Malick crafted a beautiful tale that revolves around a bizarre love triangle. Rightly praised for its spectacular cinematography, *Days Of Heaven* is a slow-burning classic that really deserves to be seen, even after all this time.

Superman The Movie

1978

62 For many, Christopher Reed will always be Superman. He gives a tremendous performance as the Man of Steel and would go on to play the role for three additional movies. Filmed back to back with its sequel (which was released in 1980) it was famous upon release for being the most expensive film of all time with an astonishing budget of $55 million.

Kramer Vs Kramer

1979

63 Robert Benton's award-winning courtroom drama not only scored the five most prestigious awards at the 52nd Academy Awards but also became the highest-grossing film of the year with over $106 million. Despite winning an Oscar, Meryl Streep wasn't originally intended for the main role, winning the role after Kate Jackson, Ali McGraw, Jane Fonda and Faye Dunaway turned it down.

Amityville Horror ▲

`1979`

64 Horror films were big business in Hollywood throughout the Seventies and Eighties and one of the most successful was this adaptation of Jay Anson's book of the same name. Made for just under $5 million it ended up earning over $86 million. Not too shabby for a movie originally planned to go straight to television. Nearly 20 sequels have followed, with the more recent ones typically going directly to streaming.

"Halloween's $70 million in takings gave Carpenter huge creative freedom for later films"

Watership Down

1978

65 Don't be fooled by the gorgeous animation and the cute fluffy rabbits on display, because *Watership Down* is a brutal adaptation of Richard Adams' hit novel, which traumatized a generation of kids. Famed for its gorgeous animation and strong voice cast (which includes John Hurt and Richard Briers), it was remade into a brand-new mini series in 2018.

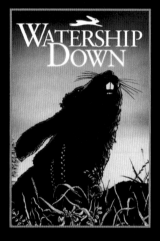

Apocalypse Now

1979

66 Few Seventies film shoots were as troublesome as *Apocalypse Now*'s. Sets were destroyed by terrible weather, Marlon Brando turned up completely unprepared for his role and lead Martin Sheen suffered a near fatal heart attack. Somehow Francis Ford Coppola not only persevered through all these mishaps (which are chronicled in the 1991 documentary *Hearts Of Darkness: A Filmmaker's Apocalypse*) but also turned it into one of the most celebrated war films of all time.

Alien

1979

67 Ridley Scott's movie remains a masterpiece in slow-building tension, and introduced cinemagoers to one of film's most iconic monsters. As much a horror as it is a science fiction film, *Alien* is elevated by its sensational cast, monumental world building and HR Giger's spectacular monster design. It has spawned countless sequels and prequels, many of which have come nowhere near Scott's stunning original.

The Jerk

1979

68 Steve Martin was already well known as a comedic performer due to his TV and stage work during the Sixties and Seventies, but it was *The Jerk* and his move into movies that led to his international fame. Often cited as one of the funniest films ever made, it's seen by many as a career best from Martin and led to a disappointing 1984 sequel, *The Jerk, Too*, which starred Mark Blankfield in Martin's original role.

The Black Hole

1979

69 After seeing the success of *Star Wars*, Disney decided to make its own space opera. Unfortunately, while it featured a strong cast and superb special effects it didn't make the same impact as George Lucas' movie. It's surprisingly dark for a Disney film and is also the first to feature (admittedly mild) swearing. A planned remake has been stuck in development hell since 2009.

Manhattan

1979

70 Woody Allen released several notable films throughout the Seventies, but this collaboration with writer Marshall Brickman, is generally considered to be his best from the era. Inspired by his love of George Gershwin's music, it's a gorgeous love letter to New York City and features an excellent cast along with sharp, well-observed writing.

Boggle has made a big enough impact in popular culture that it has popped up in some surprising places. It's referenced in *Friends*, *The Simpsons*, and *King of the Hill*.

One of the skills in Boggle is that you have to read letters that will fall into the tray upside down or to the side. It sounds easier than it is – it's all too easy to panic and confuse an M for an upside-down W, for example.

BOGGLE

Crashing, rattling, and clattering. It was a distinctive din that any Boggle-owning household would instantly recognize. It is, of course, the sound of lettered Boggle cubes being shaken around in the game's plastic shell. The cubes then fall into the 4 × 4 tray at the base of the shell, before the timer is turned and Boggle begins, as players race to find the highest-scoring word among the mess of letters.

A big part of Boggle's appeal is how easy it is to play. The rules are simple. When the timer is up, all players compare the words they have found. Any words that appear on multiple lists are eliminated, with players earning points for words that only they

have found, scoring the number of letters in each. Then there's the design of Boggle itself. The bold, punchy font of its lettering is almost as distinct as the sound of the rattling cubes denoting a new game that's about to start.

It's testament to the strength of Allan Turoff's original design that Boggle has remained the same game that hit the shelves back in 1972. The letter distribution is tweaked slightly from region to region, but otherwise there's little to tell the editions apart and there's been no evolution or redesign to the game itself. In fact, the only real difference has been that modern versions of the game are now designed with a shell and cubes that don't make quite as much noise when rattled – although it is up for debate whether losing out on the trademark noise is a good thing or not.

The white, orange and black color scheme is as big a part of Boggle, as is the distinctive font size. Despite some variants such as blue, the original color scheme has always endured since the game was first created.

THE LEGACY

Somewhat inevitably, the popularity of Boggle led to bigger versions of the same game being made. Big Boggle featured a 5 × 5 tray (with extra rules, such as three-letter words not being allowed) with Super Big Boggle following, with a 6 × 6 tray. Yet Boggle's lasting appeal is best measured by mobile phone app Ruzzle, which was inspired by the classic word game. Ruzzle topped the iPhone charts in 2013 and has been downloaded over 10 million times on Android.

A small plastic shell fits over this tray and each game begins by shaking the cubes about. The shell is clear, so you can see if the cubes have fallen into the tray.

LITTLE PROFESSOR CALCULATOR

Calculators became portable during the 1970s following a breakthrough that enabled their development using a few low-powered chips. In 1973, they also became affordable thanks, in large part, to Sinclair Cambridge, which produced a fully formed calculator for $29.95, plus one in kit form for a pocket-friendly fiver.

By 1976, however, calculators were not only allowing adults to put away their slide rules and solve complex mathematical problems, they were also encouraging children to test their mental math skills. Cue Little Professor, a calculator that worked in reverse by displaying a series of sums on a red LED display and getting the user to answer them. And if that seemed like hard work, then the book-holding cartoon character drawn on to the front of the case would surely prove appealing enough to spur kids into continuing.

Little Professor was created by Texas Instruments, and demand for the educational toy upon launch was high. It preyed on parental fears that calculators would make children lazy and the aim was to answer 10 equations correctly and get a perfect score. If the user got one wrong, "EEE" would display on the screen, prompting another try. Following the third wrong answer, the correct solution would appear and it would then move to the next equation

To spice things up, there were four levels of problem difficulty, as well as a range of activities detailed in a booklet called Fun With Math Facts, some of which required two or more players. It proved so popular that, by 1977, it had sold more than a million units. That really was some success, whichever way you do the maths.

Each Little Professor came with a manual called Fun With Math Facts that contained 18 games and activities. They were split between beginner, intermediate and advanced, with most of them involving the Little Professor in some way. You could argue that the device was one of the first handheld gaming machines!

FLYING LOOPERS

Many can play this activity. Turn the "Little Professor" ON. Switch the level of difficulty to 2 or 3. (You decide.) Push SET, = and GO. Take turns doing the multiplication problem and write the answers in the squares on the gameboard below. Then place this book, open to this page, flat on the floor up against a wall. Practice shooting rubber bands off the wall above the book until you can make them land on the gameboard. Each player shoots and counts the numbers inside his or her rubber bands. The one with the highest score wins.

FUN WITH MATH FACTS

18 LEARNING GAMES AND ACTIVITIES USING
THE LITTLE PROFESSOR™

More than 16,000 problems were pre-programmed into Little Professor and it could keep going for some time on its single nine-volt disposable battery. Texas Instruments was also keen to emphasize to parents that the first educational electronic toy never made a mistake, so they could rest assured their children would be taught well "through an enjoyable instant feedback and reinforcement situation".

Information

Manufacturer: Texas Instruments
First Released: 1976
Expect to pay: $7

The 1980 version of Little Professor reduced the size of the keys so that they no longer covered the pages of the book as they did with the 1978 model. This made it look more faithful to the original, although its innards were technologically similar to Texas Instrument's 1000 model calculator rather than the 1200 of old.

THE LEGACY

A second version of Little Professor was released in 1978 and it moved some of the functions around, placing the Level key on the front, shifting the Set button to a new top row and making the On and Off keys more noticeable. Further rejigs took place in 1980 and 1982, the latter replacing the LED display with LCD and, in the 2000s, a solar version was introduced. Little Professor continues to be sold today and there's even an Android version to be enjoyed on Google Play.

The original 1976 model placed the On/Off button on the left-hand side of the unit. It also allowed the levels to be altered using the button on the right and it kept the front of the device simple with just 16 buttons. Users would turn it on, press Set, select addition, subtraction, division or multiply, and press Go.

© TI 1976

"LITTLE PROFESSOR"™

Information

Manufacturer: Denys Fisher Toys
First Released: 1965
Expect to pay: $10

SPIROGRAPH

Polish mathematician Bruno Abakanowicz invented the Spirograph not as a toy, but as a mathematical tool he could use for calculating the area of curved spaces. The origin of the modern version that we are familiar lies with British engineer Denys Fisher, who picked up on Abakanowicz's work with the intention of helping NATO track waves to aid with bomb detection. However, Fisher soon realized his Spirograph had more potential as a toy. He took it to the 1965 Nuremberg International Toy Fair, where he sold the US distribution rights to Kenner, and followed up by launching his own company to sell the toy in the UK. It was an instant hit.

A simple collection of plastic-toothed wheels combined with gears that run along those teeth, Spirograph allowed kids to easily create incredible geometric drawings, rolling their pens smoothly around the rings as intricate patterns gradually revealed themselves with a hypnotic beauty. Even with no artistic talent, you could create something that looked amazing, whether by following the instructions that came with the toy, or by freestyling to explore the millions of artistic possibilities on offer for the creative spirographer.

With the toy's success, Spirograph sets were continually evolving, adding a variety of new tools and gears, which you will no doubt remember from your own Spirograph set. It kept on selling, to the point that almost everyone had one in the 1970's, making it one of the decade's most iconic toys.

Spirograph was named Toy of the Year in 1967. More than 45 years later in 2014, it was again a Toy of the Year finalist in two categories. That longevity shows you just what a special toy the Spirograph is and why it took the 1970s by storm.

There has been a whole variety of updated sets over the years, some simply adding more gears of different sizes and some adding gears of different shapes, along with additional tools that open up new artistic possibilities.

The curved shapes you can create by rolling around the outside teeth of a Spirograph wheel are technically known as epitrochoids. Shapes that you create by rolling around the inside of a circle with your Spirograph tools are called hypotrochoids.

THE LEGACY

The 1970s generation is not the only one to have a strong affinity with the Spirograph. Clearly, there's something appealing at its core, because it has enjoyed an enduring popularity that kept it selling into the 80s, 90s and beyond. You can still buy Spirograph sets today. It has even been embraced by artists such as Judy Pfaff, Jeffrey Simmons and Ian Dawson, who have exhibited Spirograph-created or influenced art in gallery shows.

BAER'S ODYSSEY

The 1970s marked the release of the first ever games console, Ralph Baer's amazing Magnavox Odyssey

Conceptual, TV Gaming Display

It was a nice sunny day," recalls Ralph Baer, of 2 June 1976. "He was with his lawyer. We shook hands, exchanged a few pleasantries and that was it. A smile, a hello and a goodbye. That was the first time I met Nolan Bushnell."

It was a brief encounter outside the Chicago Federal District Court Building, yet a quietly momentous one in the history of videogames. Not only was Magnavox, the manufacturers of the first videogame console, about to sue Atari over *Pong*-related patent infringement, this was the first meeting of the two founding fathers of the games industry. Nolan, who with Atari had made arcade videogames a part of popular culture, and Ralph, whose pioneering work in the Sixties led to the creation of the Odyssey games console in 1972, which turned our televisions into playfields. Here, we look back at Ralph's journey, and salute the father of home videogames.

1946 – First serve?

"My brother in law, Walter, swears I had a bouncing ball on my oscilloscope back in 1946," Ralph begins. "I have zero recollection of it but I bet you dollars to doughnuts that I wasn't the only one playing with their 'scope at that time, making spots bounce back and forth on the X-Y display. If he saw it or if he didn't, it really doesn't make any difference in the history of videogames."

So we'll sadly never know for certain whether a very primitive *Pong* ever played out on Ralph's tiny oscilloscope screen, 12 years before Willy Higginbotham's *Tennis for Two* briefly wowed visitors to Brookhaven National Labs in 1958. His brother's memory does, however, demonstrate Ralph's keen interest electronics. Coming from

a Jewish background, he and his family fled Germany in 1938, just two months before the Nazi's savage anti-Semitic Kristallnacht pogrom. They settled in New York, and Ralph spent three years serving in the US Army, both stateside and overseas. He put his electronics expertise to good effect; "When I was with military intelligence, one of the first things I did when we got to Europe was build a radio for the guy who I shared a bunk with. I managed to convert German mine detectors so we could pick up the American Forces Radio Station and listen to Glenn Miller."

After the war ended, Ralph took advantage of the G.I. Bill of Rights and went to college in Chicago. Graduating in 1949 with a Bachelor of Science in Television Engineering (the first degree available of this kind at the time), he would soon get the chance to make a TV set of his own.

1951 – 'That's kind of neat'

In 1951, Ralph was gainfully employed at Loral, an electronics company based in the Bronx, working on a high-class projection television set. "Part of the test equipment we used as we built the set was a pattern generator," he recalls. "You could put a pattern on-screen, like a checkerboard, so you could test the height, width, contrast, brightness, that kind of thing… I said, 'That's kind of neat, you can fiddle with these controls and things happen on the screen. Couldn't we build something like this into a television set and make it into some kind of game?' I took the idea to my supervisor and he said, 'You're already behind schedule, just get the damn TV set built!' And that was the end of that!"

The name of Ralph's supervisor? Sam Lackoff. We can't help wondering, if it

» The famous Brown Box and rifle, with the tangle of wires within that made the magic happen.

» Ralph with his Telesketch console in 1975.

weren't for his lack of vision could we have been playing games on our televisions in the Fifties instead of the Seventies? "No question about it," states Ralph, emphatically. "Technically, no problem whatsoever. If it would've resulted in a saleable product that did enough for whatever it would cost, well, that's a question I can't answer."

Just imagine if the industry had started 20 years earlier than it did. Where would we be now?

sports games, even "Auto Racing using the screen as a roadway". Before a spot was even displayed, Ralph was planning what we might actually be playing in this brave new gaming world.

"What's wrong with looking ahead?" he laughs. "I was thinking of what I could do with this thing! I knew there were 40 million TV sets in the United States. If I could hook up some kind of box to a TV set that did something

"I bet you dollars to doughnuts that I wasn't the only one playing with their 'scope at that time, making spots bounce back and forth on the X-Y display"

1966 – Do the Bus Stop

15 years had passed since Ralph first toyed with the notion of playing games on a television. Since then, he'd moved to Sanders Associates and risen up the ranks to chief engineer, working mainly on military defence electronics projects, but his inner 'TV gamer' had never died. "I was waiting at a New York bus terminal for a colleague and it just came back to me," smiles Ralph. "The idea of playing games on a TV set had always been just under the surface. I remember sitting on a cement step outside the terminal, scribbling notes on a small pad. I got that feeling of being on to something…"

When he returned to his office in New Hampshire the following day, he wrote up his New York notes into a four-page document that laid out his ideas for playing games on a conventional television set. It's a fascinating piece of videogaming history because not only does it contain talk of oscillators, modulators, 'free-running raster techniques' and the numerous practicalities of actually getting images on screen, it talks about games. Action games, card games,

that people would want to pay for and I could sell that to just 1 percent of TV owners, that's 400,000 right there! I got a business! Then there's the rest of the world. That's gotta be another 40 or 50 million, right?"

Ralph was thinking big, which might explain why he clearly stated in the document that development should take place 'in a guarded and otherwise inaccessible room', with 'disclosure confined to a minimum of personnel.' He also had the presence of mind to get the seminal document signed and dated by a trusted colleague, Bob Solomon, to establish a legal record of his eureka moment, a highly prescient move given the slew of lawsuits that would follow over the following decades. Ralph must have instantly realized this was an important breakthrough. Something big, something worth protecting…

"There was no question in my mind," he confirms. "Of course, I could never have known how big it would really get…."

Realizing the potential was one thing; making it become reality was to be an arduous,

All items shown on these two pages are regularly-priced, with no Annual Sale Savings

ODYSSEY

… the electronic game of the future. A total play and learning experience for all ages!

ODYSSEY is the fantastic new electronic game that easily attaches to any brand 18 to 25 inch (diagonal) television to create a closed circuit electronic playground. With **ODYSSEY** you participate in television . . . you're not just a spectator! The fascinating casino action of Monte Carlo, the excitement of Wimbledon, the thrills of a heated game of football—can all be duplicated right in your own living room!

ODYSSEY is thought, action and reaction. **ODYSSEY** comes complete with a battery-powered master control unit (batteries included), six printed circuit game cards, twelve action and learning games for the entire family, eleven different game overlays and two player controls, as well as a wide variety of game aids. The master unit allows you to control the speed of the game; the player control lets **ODYSSEY** you move your player vertically, horizontally and even apply "English."

ODYSSEY is also an electronic teaching aid. Your child can learn numbers, letters, geography even abstract thinking! And best of all, **ODYSSEY** makes learning fun.

ODYSSEY . . . it's new from Magnavox . . . and works with any brand TV—black and white or color. Come in now for the fun of a demonstration. **ODYSSEY**—model 1TL200.

$99.95

47

elongated struggle. It began by Ralph assigning a technician, Bob Tremblay, to his secret project. Ensconced in the former company library on the fifth floor, out of sight from any curious eyes, Bob (under Ralph's direction) created a vacuum-tube circuit, which was christened TV Game Unit 1. So, did tense games of ping-pong between the

two of them soon follow? Ralph laughs out loud at the thought. "No, no, it couldn't do a hell of a lot! It could put a spot on the screen and stretch it vertically, horizontally, move it around and change its color. It wasn't meant to be a product but it proved we could get symbols on screen and that was the purpose of the exercise…"

That tiny tangle of wires and tubes was the 'proof of concept' that Ralph needed. He approached the company's corporate director of research and development, Herbert Campman, and gave a demonstration of the unit. This time, Ralph's superior had vision, and on 22 December 1966, he agreed to fund further development: $2000 for direct labor and $500 for materials. Now that he project had a little cash, and some credence from the company's management., it was game on.

» An overlay for *Prehistoric Safari* – the *Dino Crisis* of the early Seventies.

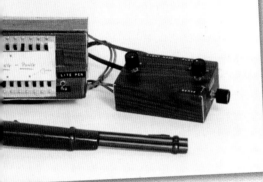

1967 – A Tale of Two Bills

The new year brought two additions to Ralph's team. Two very different men that would in very different ways play vital roles in the creation of the first ever games console.

"Bill Harrison was my kind of guy," says Ralph. "He was a really good technician. He became an engineer later on, and he designed all the circuitry. He was on the bench, while I was out there running a division of five hundred people. I'd stick my head in a couple of times a day for 15 minutes to see how things were going. He worked under my direction but he did the work and

came up with stuff that we could manufacture and was inexpensive. For example, to generate a spot to move around a screen like for a ping-pong game, to do that in discrete logic typically takes four transistors. He did it in two. Once you need three spots, for two bats and a ball, that's a lot fewer transistors and resistors and that's saving you money."

So on 12 February 1967, Ralph took Bill to the same secretive room where Bob Tremblay had put together TV Game Unit 1, and he began working on what would become the second iteration of their game-changing console adventure.

Meanwhile, Ralph began sharing his game ideas with one of Herb Campman's engineers, Bill Rusch. "He was an MIT graduate," explains Ralph. "Very bright, very creative and very eccentric. He'd go out at lunch to play his guitar to people I thought were groupies. He was very independent and wouldn't take direction, but I tolerated it because he was very useful. A million times I would've cheerfully let him go if he wasn't such an important contributor to the effort."

That contribution can be clearly seen in a memo dated 10 May 1967. It detailed 21 different videogames, a culmination of conversations between Rusch and Ralph over the previous three months about what their TV game unit might be able to deliver. It reads like a manifesto for future game genres: there's a top down racing game where circuit-crashes or rear-ending the race leader are penalized; a baseball game where the speed of the pitch can be controlled and the batter must time their swing perfectly to make a hit; a maze game in which a white rat must traverse a labyrinth; various target-shooting games; and an idea for an aerial World War One dogfighting duel, pre-empting Atari's ubiquitous *Combat* cartridge by a decade. There are even plans for an intriguing golf game that resulted in a bizarre peripheral.

"We built joysticks for Game Unit 2," explains Ralph, speaking about the practical aspects of implementing some of their game ideas. "What's more obvious to an engineer like me than to drill a hole in a golf ball and stick it on a joystick? Put it on the floor and hit it with your putter. Get it right and you get a hole in one!"

$$Q: \sqrt{A^2 + B^2} = ?$$

» Ralph demonstrates the Odyssey 200 console, released in 1975.

» Ralph takes aim using a *Brown Box* rifle.

Mid-1967 – Summer of Games

Full of ideas and with an encouraging number of incremental technical breakthroughs, the group prepared to showcase their progress to the president of the company, Royden Sanders, and the board of directors. "I knew I couldn't blow this," says Ralph, "so I recorded the instructions for the games on Game Unit 2 on audio tape and I had Bill Harrison build a little 4.5 MHz oscillator and modulator so the sound came through the television set. I switched it on and, for the first time in human history, we had a videogame running with verbal instructions coming out of the TV."

Seven games were demoed to the board that day. *Fox and Hounds*, a two player chase game, had a single red spot for a 'fox', pursued by three white 'hounds', while *Target Shooting* allowed one player to move the bullseye with the joystick, as a second tried to blast it with his rifle. Most intriguing was *Pumping Game*, in which the player took on the role of a firefighter frantically trying to extinguish the flames in a burning house, success being achieved by pumping a handle on the console. This primitive button-basher was accompanied by a charming hand-drawn overlay, featuring a determined fireman gripping his hose. The windows of the building were transparent, allowing the player to see the opposing levels of red (fire) and blue (water) color on screen, which indicated success or failure at the task.

So, did the board see the germ of a multi-billion dollar industry in those seven videogame vignettes? "They said I was nuts!" exclaims Ralph. "We were a military electronics company building very complex, very expensive equipment, like anti-aircraft to ground missile protection. This was a long, long way from that. The reception was actually pretty cold. Out of the whole group, only two were smiling after the demo was done and they became supporters. The rest looked pretty dumb. But I guess they trusted me. I had been around a while…"

The truth was, Ralph and his team were also starting to have doubts. Their games were fun, but their lasting appeal was questionable.

There was only so much entertainment you could squeeze out of two spots chasing each other across the screen, however cleverly you dressed it up. Then in November came a major breakthrough. Bill Rusch designed some novel spot generator circuitry on paper, Bill Harrison implemented it and now a third spot could be displayed on screen. This spot was different; it was machine controlled, and therefore, most excitingly, it could be a 'ball'.

"It was obvious we finally had something worth going after," enthuses Ralph, warming to the subject. "I mean, the other games, we were dragging them in by the hair just to have something to do but as soon as we had a ping-pong game, that was of a totally different order."

And so the first 'killer app' was born. All that had to be done was to turn the game into something they could sell to the world.

1969 – Boxing Clever

Videogame Unit 7 was given the name of the Brown Box, so called because the aluminium chassis containing the game circuitry was now covered with brown, self-adhesive wood-grain vinyl. This box of tricks could play various kinds of ping-pong, all developed by the team over the previous year. Volleyball, soccer and hockey all played around with the same basic 'two bats, one ball' formula, some utilizing overlays to add goals and other little touches of 'realism' to proceedings. The light-gun and golf-putting games made the final cut, along with a version of checkers. Herb Campman's response confirmed the team's hopes: "This looks like it's for real."

"No question it was ready to produce," says Ralph, "But we had to figure out who was going to put it into production! We had been trying to get cable companies interested but they just didn't have the guts. I can't believe it took us a whole year to realize all the parts we were using were the same parts used by TV and radio manufacturers. Those were who we needed to be talking to! And they came, one by one, and all of them said, Gee, this is great, but did any of 'em move off a dime? No. RCA was the only one who put together

The big guns come out

"WHAT DO YOU do with a single spot on a screen?" muses Ralph. "It's pretty boring, right? So you shoot it! As soon as that idea came along, I sent Bill Harrison out to buy a plastic rifle. Opened it up, found room to put some electronics in – a sensor, some amplification, a little coincidence circuitry – so when you pull the trigger, and you're lined up with that source of light on the screen, the spot, you get a hit and you make that hit turn off the spot so it disappears."

Thus in 1967, a light-gun game was implemented for TV Game Unit 2, and another long-running videogame genre was established. We wonder whether the idea of adding a gun to the project might have come from the fact that Sanders was involved primarily in the defence industry or perhaps it was a reflection of America's well-established gun culture?

Ralph is quick to respond. "This comes up so often. You see these documentaries on the history of videogames and they make a big deal about this relationship with the military. I don't think it had a damn thing to do with it. A kid that goes to a carnival, does he have a go at skeet shooting because his dad was in the army? No, it's because it's freakin' fun!"

» A selection of the many games and toys Ralph has worked on over the years.

Simon says

OF RALPH'S NUMEROUS post-Odyssey creations, the most commercially successful was the iconic handheld Simon. The simple 'follow the notes' gameplay, and stylish, circular design led to sales of several million units and versions of the handheld still remain in production today, 40 years after its launch in 1978.

"It was just serendipity that *Close Encounters of the Third Kind* was out," recalls Ralph. "The mothership was round and made sounds like Simon. When I saw the movie I said, Hey it's Simon coming in! I'm sure, subliminally, it helped sales."

Simon has a special place in Ralph's heart, and it's not just due to its lasting popularity. The idea for the game originated after he had played an old Atari arcade game called *Touch Me* at a trade show, a game that was supposedly born from a concept by Nolan Bushnell himself.

"We managed to make a real success of Simon and so, unintentionally, I managed to upstage Nolan for once," chuckles Ralph.

You can read more about the Simon handheld game on p90.

a contract and that took three months and it was so onerous to us that we walked away. But we got lucky. One of the RCA guys left to join Magnavox and told them they should take another look at us. We presented [the Brown Box] to them and their manager said, 'Go!' That's how it all started."

1972 – The Best Medicine

It's the summer of '72 and Ralph is lying in a hospital bed, recovering from a routine operation. The high of 1969 seems a long time ago. Since their TV game was given the green light, things had been moving slowly. A year to sort out the legal contracts and another for the Brown Box prototype to be manufactured into the Magnavox Odyssey, which finally hit the shelves in the summer of 1972. Worse still, Sanders was hit badly by a severe slump in the defence industry, resulting in large-scale job losses at the company. In his own words, Ralph was in a 'deep funk'.

"You can't compare the technology I had back in the Sixties with what we have today. I look at my iPad and it's magic! Bloody magic!"

"You can read all the books on psychology you want, the reason people get depressed is that they lose confidence in themselves," he reasons. "My division in the company had shrunk by a few hundred people, employees were hiding behind storage cabinets to avoid getting on the lay-offs list and I was in hospital for this operation. Then in walks Herb Campman with a giant check for $100,000! That was substantial money back then, like $300,000 in today's dollars. It was like someone had turned a switch on in me. In a micro-second I went from depression to elation!"

That three-foot photocopy of the first royalty check received by Sanders for sales of the Odyssey console was tangible proof of what Ralph and his tiny team had always believed: people would love videogames.

That Christmas, 100,000 consoles were sold and the Magnavox Odyssey went on to sell 350,000 units over the next few years.

"In terms of selling a brand new product it was an unqualified success," beams Ralph. "It didn't matter that by the time it came out it was old technology. It worked and it was fun. And you know, it owed much of its success to the fact that Atari had brought out their copy of it, *Pong*, in the arcades. You wanna play that at home, you go buy a Magnavox Odyssey game. And that's what people did…"

Success inevitably breeds imitation. Atari had built their arcade business from the huge profits generated by *Pong*, which did indeed bear an uncanny resemblance to the Odyssey's ping-pong game. Countless other Johnny-come-latelys also jumped on the bandwagon and produced home and arcade versions of the game. In 1975, Atari decided to produce a home version of their arcade hit and so we return to those courthouse steps in Chicago…

1976 – Who's the Daddy?

"I felt confident from the start," says Ralph. "Nolan had played our game at a Magnavox dealership in Burlingame, California, in May '72. No-one can tell me that wasn't the inspiration for him to tell Al Alcorn to build *Pong*. That's fine. I've been in the toy and game business long enough to know everyone bases their ideas on other people's. Nothing comes from a vacuum. But we had issued patents that had clearly been infringed by Atari and others."

The judge agreed and Magnavox – and by extension, Ralph – won on all counts. Well, all but one, perhaps. For many years, as the videogame industry boomed, and occasionally busted, into the billion-dollar business it is today, it was Nolan who was

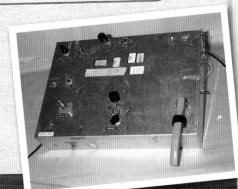

» The Magnavox Odyssey, the world's first console.

Still creating after all these years...

From Coleco's Telstar and Kid-Vid series, Ralph has been involved in literally hundreds of innovative projects, ranging from interactive toys for children to talking greetings cards. And despite being in his 90th year at the time of this interview, he has no intention of stopping.

"As we're speaking, my marketing guy is on his way to California to present two products we've just finished to a company in the Bay area," explains Ralph proudly. "I've got better at doing at my own software and I've done dozens of games over the last few years. One of the projects is a talking book, where a kid can store their own voice and play around with it, and the other is a tricycle with electronics added in that turn it into a games machine!" he enthuses.

Mobile gaming the Baer way. More power to his soldering iron and his endless imagination.

referred to as the father of videogames. Ralph's role was largely ignored and his huge contribution to the birth of the hobby went unacknowledged for several years. Thankfully, the wonderful web helped put the story straight.

"I was a no-show before the internet," sighs Ralph. "Then I got a website and that put me on the map. Since then, I've received the National Medal of Technology from President Bush, the original Brown Box is in the Smithsonian Museum and I've been awarded so many prizes and medals, I don't know what to do with them all. They're cluttering up my desk here! The amount of emails I get from students with yards of questions to help them with a paper they're writing on the history of videogames, maybe that's an indication that I've finally arrived!"

Before we leave Ralph to get back to work at his bench in his basement lab, we wonder whether he ever looks at what videogames

have become, both commercially and culturally, and thinks, did I really start this? He thinks a while before answering.

"Well, obviously, yes, but I'm very conscious that though I might have started it, there are thousands of creative people that made it all happen. And you can't compare the technology that I had back in the Sixties with what we have today. I look at my iPad and it's magic! Bloody magic! And everything's only getting more magical!"

So gamers, raise your joysticks to the wizard that cast the first spell. To Ralph Baer, the true Father of Videogames.

A special thank you to Ralph for providing the images for this article. You can order his fascinating book Videogames: In The Beginning *from www.rolentapress.com and find out more about his incredible career at www.ralphbaer.com Additional images courtesy of David Winter of www.pong-story.com*

» Ralph with one of the latest versions of his ever-popular handheld, *Simon.*

» This overlay for the early *Pumping Game* was hand drawn by Stew Gregory, a draftsman at Sanders.

THE LEGACY

Weebles remain popular today and have been given the standard licensing treatment, emerging in themes including Peppa Pig, various Disney characters, the Teletubbies and Paw Patrol. The newer versions tend to be far more detailed that the originals, but the principles behind them remain the same. In 1978 a variant was released called the 'Tumblin' Weebles', in which the weight was loose and allowed the Weeble to move more freely and even (shock) fall over. Needless to say, they didn't catch on.

▼

The Weeble concept has been used in other countries, such as Japan, where weighted papier-mâché toys are known as 'okiagari-koboshi'. In Spain, 'Los Weebles' were manufactured by Brekar and the name itself may derive from the Dutch word for wobble – 'wiebelen', which is pronounced 'weebelen'.

▲

Experts in child development say that 'roly-poly' toys like Weebles help youngsters develop their motor skills, because the toy does not roll out of reach when given a swipe, meaning that Weebles are educational as well as fun.

Weebles figures, playground, dolls' house and family, 1973
'Weebles wobble, but they don't fall down' – because of their weighted bases. They grow wegetables and drive weehicles. Made in England by Airfix Products Ltd.

WEEBLES

Kids love a challenge, and when a toy comes along with a jingle claiming that "Weebles wobble but they don't fall down", then the gauntlet has well and truly been thrown down.

The truth of the matter, however, was that Weebles really lived up to their publicity – wobbling with the slightest provocation but refusing to actually topple over. The secret lay in the construction, which used a weighted bottom to keep the egg-shaped characters from staying in a prone position.

Originally produced by Romper Room, the company behind a successful American kids TV show of the same name, the brand was bought by Hasbro's Playskool division in the early 1970s.

The earliest versions of the toy were basic egg shapes with stickers to add characterisation. With family values at the heart of the brand, the first Weebles were a mum and dad, along with two children, a baby and a family dog. Playsets followed as the Weebles proved a hit, and kids could soon enjoy all sorts of fun with a tree house, a boat, a plane, a playground, a circus and more. More than 40 sets were developed and marketed during the toy's 1970s heyday.

In the UK, Weebles were marketed by Airfix and had a distinctly different appearance. In fact, they were downright demonic, with molded plastic features in contrast to the stickers on the American version. Despite their questionable looks and sunken eyes, however, the UK Weebles also proved popular with the kids.

Ages 2-7

One of the most popular of the 1970s playsets featured a haunted house, complete with a glow-in-the-dark Weeble ghost that could be dropped down the chimney to emerge in a fireplace. The set was completed with a witch figure and two 'scared' children (it wasn't really very scary).

Information

Manufacturer: Romper Room/ Playskool
First Released: 1969
Expect to pay: $5

There is a rumor that the idea for Weebles came from an inflatable clown in the TV show Romper Room, which could be punched, but which would always bounce back. Whether or not the range of loveable Weebles actually had such a violent origin story is debatable, but the inflatable clown was also released as a toy.

© Alamy, Getty Images

EVEL KNIEVEL STUNT CYCLE

Many children of the 1970s will fondly recall Robert Craig Knievel Jr – better known as the American stunt performer Evel Knievel. On May 26, 1975, 90,000 people at Wembley Stadium watched his attempt to leap over 13 single-decker buses. He failed, breaking his pelvis in the process and vowing never to jump again (he did). But if that didn't get the adrenaline going, then being able to recreate those stunts at home did.

Luckily for parents, the Evel Knievel Stunt Cycle posed no danger to their offspring. Instead, the toy was a mini plastic Knievel astride his infamous bike and a separate contraption for the back wheel to connect into. By turning a handle on this so-called "energizer", a revving noise would fill the air. Then, within a very short amount of time, enough momentum would be built to allow Evel to be released. The bike shot off at speed to deal with whatever obstacles were in its path.

Created by Ideal Toys and part of a best-selling Evel Knievel range, the idea was you'd be able to set up ramps, ditches and rows of toy vehicles for the tiny stuntman to tackle. In truth, the toy would generally smash into the skirting board or flop on to its side with the back wheel spinning wildly. Yet it was still very cool and desirable and, with a bit of practice, you could have it whipping over your Christmas annuals and over carefully laid-out Action Men in no time.

Information

Manufacturer: Ideal Toys
First Released: 1973
Expect to pay: $90

▶

The Evel Knievel figure was bendable and it came complete with a costume made out of cloth. It was also possible to remove the helmet and belt. Some people have commented that their Evel's head came off during their stunts. But then it was a rough and tumble toy.

THE LEGACY

Ideal Toys stopped making Knievel merchandise in 1977 but by that time the range had made a whopping $125 million. By then the entertainer had begun to limit his appearances and his last show took place in 1980. Despite that, reissued Knievel toys appeared in the late 1990s and 2000s including a new Super Stunt Cycle Set by POOF-Slinky that included a dragster and car. Such is Evel's legacy and attractiveness of the original Stunt Cycle that toys in good condition can now fetch a tidy sum.

▲

The original gyro-powered Evel Knievel Stunt Cycle in the first half of 1973 was created using chrome parts. These were removed from the front forks during subsequent production runs to reduce the cost of manufacturing. Those that have them are the rarest and most valuable of the entire range.

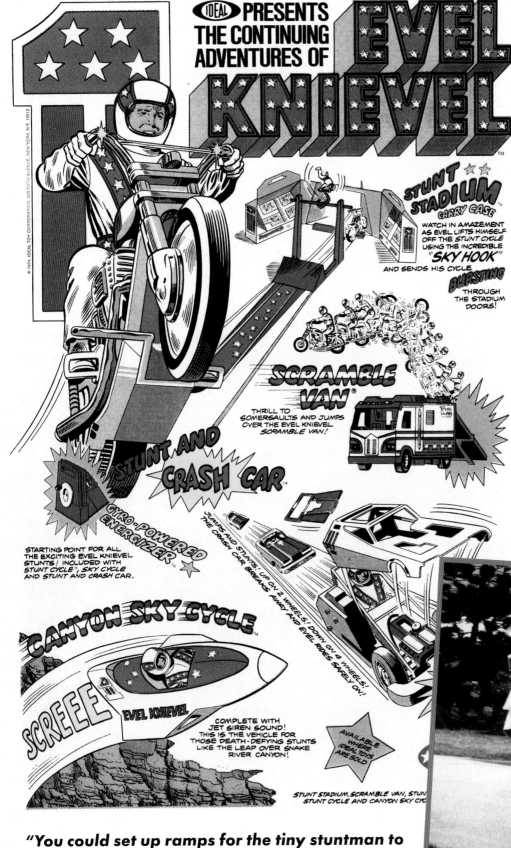

IDEAL PRESENTS THE CONTINUING ADVENTURES OF EVEL KNIEVEL™

© 1974 IDEAL TOY CORPORATION 200 FIFTH AVENUE, NEW YORK, N.Y. 10010

STUNT STADIUM™ CARRY CASE™
WATCH IN AMAZEMENT AS EVEL LIFTS HIMSELF OFF THE STUNT CYCLE USING THE INCREDIBLE "SKY HOOK" AND SENDS HIS CYCLE BURSTING THROUGH THE STADIUM DOORS!

SCRAMBLE VAN®
THRILL TO SOMERSAULTS AND JUMPS OVER THE EVEL KNIEVEL SCRAMBLE VAN!

STUNT AND CRASH CAR™
JUMPS AND STUNTS! UP ON 2 WHEELS! DOWN ON 4 WHEELS! THE CRASH CAR BREAKS AWAY AND EVEL RIDES SAFELY ON!

GYRO-POWERED ENERGIZER™
STARTING POINT FOR ALL THE EXCITING EVEL KNIEVEL STUNTS! INCLUDED WITH STUNT CYCLE, SKY CYCLE AND STUNT AND CRASH CAR.

CANYON SKY CYCLE™
SCREEE
EVEL KNIEVEL
COMPLETE WITH JET SIREN SOUND! THIS IS THE VEHICLE FOR THOSE DEATH-DEFYING STUNTS LIKE THE LEAP OVER SNAKE RIVER CANYON!

AVAILABLE WHERE IDEAL TOYS ARE SOLD

STUNT STADIUM, SCRAMBLE VAN, STUN[...] STUNT CYCLE AND CANYON SKY CY[...]

"You could set up ramps for the tiny stuntman to tackle. In truth, it would flop on its side, wheel spinning wildly"

◄ The toy went through numerous variations during its lifespan in the 1970s but the way it worked remained the same. The fun in every case relied on imagination: it was all about getting Evel Knievel to perform the most stunning of stunts using whatever you had to hand. It was a toy that everyone wanted to play with.

◄ The energizer unit that sent Evel on his way came in red, blue, white, yellow and orange, though it was not clear on the box which color you would get. At least it meant that you could avoid mixing up your toys with friends when you tried to put a few Knievels head-to-head.

FEELING THE FORCE:
A STAR WARS RETROSPECTIVE

Even George Lucas wasn't sure Star Wars would be a success while he was working on it, but it went on to become one of the most important franchises of all time. Join us as we examine the many facets of the galaxy far, far away...

With the frenzied excitement that surrounded *Star Wars: The Last Jedi*, it's hard to imagine that George Lucas's original idea for his epic space saga was passed over by several big film companies. Nevertheless that's exactly what happened, with the likes of Universal Pictures, United Artists and (ironically) Disney all passing on the proposed project before 20th Century Fox finally gave it the green light.

Star Wars is now one of the biggest movie franchises in the world, and it helped turn the likes of Mark Hamill, Harrison Ford and the late Carrie Fisher into household names. Its tremendous impact in 1977 helped create what's now known as the 'Summer Blockbuster' and it has become a huge part of our pop culture, referenced in countless films and TV shows. Relentless reissues have ensured that the movies continue to inspire new generations and you'll see just as many kids today pretending to use the Force to move things as they did during the late Seventies and early Eighties.

When Ben Kenobi told Luke Skywalker about the Force, he explained that "it surrounds us and penetrates us; it binds the galaxy together". That could equally apply to the love that fans feel for the Star Wars franchise itself. For many, Star Wars is not just a set of movies, it's a code of conduct to live by. In a 2002 New Zealand survey, 53,000 residents – 1.5 percent of the county's population – stated their religion as Jedi. Even if it was just in jest, it highlights the sheer reach of Lucas's franchise.

Star Wars extends far beyond its core movies too. Lucas created a tremendously expansive universe that saw novels, cartoons and even videogames build upon the galaxy that he first dreamt up in the Seventies. Talented writers like Timothy Zahn and RA Salvatore expanded the universe massively at the beginning of the Nineties, killing off popular characters while resurrecting others. And the mythology only grew with time, eventually becoming so confusing that Disney decided that the 'Expanded Universe' would be considered non-canon going forward.

We've now come full circle, with the successful revival of the Star Wars brand in *The Force Awakens* restoring it to the very forefront of pop culture once again. Join us now, as we look at the many aspects of George Lucas's vision that have helped turn Star Wars into one of the most successful franchises the galaxy has ever known.

Obi-Wan Kenobi with a hologram in *Star Wars*.

FILMS

Star Wars sprang from Lucas's desire to create another classic sci-fi franchise

For many, the original Star Wars trilogy represents the pinnacle of George Lucas's career. They have a heart and soul that were largely missing from his three later movies and were demonstrably made by a visionary director who would stop at nothing to ensure that his planned trilogy was as uncompromised as possible. And yet, if it weren't for *THX 1138*, the trilogy and everything that came after may never have happened.

While his *THX 1138* debut movie wasn't as successful on release as Lucas had hoped, it did lead to a two-picture development deal with United Artists. One of those films would be *American Graffiti*; the other was to be based on *Flash Gordon*. Lucas was unable to obtain the rights, however, and so simply decided to make his own Flash Gordon-style movie instead. Unfortunately, studios weren't keen to buy into his vision, and he went through several before eventually landing a deal with 20th Century Fox.

Filming *Star Wars* wouldn't be easy, however. Lucas had continual disputes with his cinematographer Gilbert Taylor and had to rely heavily on his own special effects company, Industrial Light & Magic, due to Fox having disbanded its own studio. Filming at Elstree Studios in London had strict working conditions that Lucas wasn't used to and many of the crew didn't take the project seriously. Even Harrison Ford has been famously

The first big battle in *Empire* takes place on the ice planet Hoth and is still a joy to watch.

"Even today, Empire is widely considered to be the best movie in the Star Wars canon"

quoted as saying "You can type this shit, George, but you can't say it." Lucas was diagnosed with exhaustion and hypertension while Mark Hamill had a car accident which affected re-shoots. Post-production was no better, with early cuts of the film not pleasing Lucas and Industrial Light & Magic struggling to create the ground-breaking special effects. When an early cut was screened to Fox officials and several high-ranking directors – including Steven Spielberg and Brian De Palma – the screening divided the audience, and Lucas eventually found himself compromising on his original vision, in large part due to the project already being $2 million over budget.

All the pain was worth it, though, for when *Star Wars* launched in 1977, it hit with all the power and precision of Luke Skywalker's final assault on the Death Star. It was met with a rapturous reception, even if it wasn't the most original of stories – it was heavily inspired by the Japanese classic *The Hidden Fortress* – and it broke box office records. It was so wildly successful, it led to a sequel, *The Empire Strikes Back*, which arrived three years later, in 1980.

Even today, *Empire* is widely

considered to be the best movie in the Star Wars canon. While Lucas still created the original story, he passed directing duties over to Irvin Kershner, whose last film had been *The Eyes Of Laura Mars*. Leigh Brackett and Lawrence Kasdan produced the sparkling screenplay and as a result it's a far snappier film than its predecessor, building on the relationships Lucas hinted at in *Star Wars* and delivering countless lines of memorable dialogue. It was technically astonishing, too, with incredible state-of-the-art effects (it's telling that the Yoda of *Empire* feels far more realistic than his later CGI incarnations) and one of the greatest

cliff-hangers of all time.

Return of the Jedi followed three years after Empire. Kasden continued to polish Lucas's story and it concludes the original trilogy in a satisfying manner, particularly by featuring one of the greatest space battles ever committed to celluloid. Directed by the late Richard Marquand, additions such as the Ewoks led many to cynically suggest that the film was more a way of expanding Lucas's successful toy merchandising, which was making obscene amounts of money. Cash-in or not, *Jedi* was a fitting end to the trilogy, and like *Star Wars* and *Empire* before it, it still holds up incredibly well today.

Jedi was originally going to feature Chewbacca's home planet, but Lucas instead chose to introduce the cute Ewoks.

TOYS

We revisit the origins behind the classic
Star Wars toys we all enjoyed as kids

Look for these new toys from STAR WARS: RETURN OF THE JEDI collection in your favorite stores. (U.S.A. only)

SY SNOOTLES AND THE REBO BAND | EWOK - COMBAT GLIDER | EWOK - ASSAULT CATAPULT | RANCOR MONSTER

ACTION FIGURES SOLD SEPARATELY

Even before George Lucas sold Lucasfilm to Disney for $4.06bn, he was incredibly wealthy. When Lucas first began pitching *Star Wars*, he also had the idea to create a successful merchandising brand to go alongside it.

Lucas eventually received an offer from Kenner. While its president Bernie Loomis saw an opportunity, particularly for 3.75-inch figures, he, like everyone else, was caught completely by surprise by the brand's success. Always the shrewd business negotiator, Lucas passed up an extra $500,000 for a director's fee to keep control of the merchandising and licensing business. The move would end up costing Fox billions.

Kenner began to panic towards the end of 1977 when it realized how successful Star Wars was because it had no toys ready for the lucrative Christmas period. As a result, it opted to sell a redeemable voucher called The Early Bird Certificate which would allow kids to send off for Chewbacca, Princess Leia, Luke Skywalker and R2-D2 when the figures were available the following year. Kenner sold 500,000 vouchers at $7.99 apiece. The Star Wars toy line had begun…

Eight additional figures joined the original four, including Han Solo, Ben Kenobi, Darth Vader, C-3PO and Jawa. Several playsets and vehicles were also released at the end of the Seventies, including the Millennium Falcon, TIE Fighter, Landspeeder and Death Star. The Leicestershire-based toy company Palitoy would win the rights to releasing Star Wars toys in the UK and even introduced variations that weren't found in the original Kenner brand, with its cardboard and now highly coveted Death Star being one of the most notable examples.

Kenner's new toy line generated over $100 million in its first year alone and the range continued to generate millions more as additional toys and ever-more elaborate playsets were released.

"Lucas passed up an extra $500,000 for a director's fee to keep control of the merchandising"

Clever mail-order promotions like the ability to buy an early version of Boba Fett if you sent in four proof-of-purchase stamps would continue to generate excitement, while the new films generated further momentum, introducing extra figures, playsets and vehicles like the AT-AT and Ewok Village.

In total, Kenner released around 100 action figures during a nine-year period, giving full-set collectors plenty to aim for. As the brand wound down in 1985, Kenner began releasing toys under a new brand called Power Of The Force, which included a special collector's coin. In addition to repackaging many older figures, 15 final figures were added, from a carbonite-encased Han Solo to Luke Skywalker in his Stormtrooper get-up, all of which can now fetch huge prices on the collector's market.

Ten years after the original Star Wars range ended, Hasbro/Kenner resurrected the toy line in 1995 with a range of better-detailed but more muscular figures (possibly in response to the successful Masters Of The Universe range), though the uglier style would be toned down. As well as remolding several classic figures, they also renamed many to tie in with characters from the new 'Expanded Universe'. The range remained popular for five years, eventually finishing in 2000.

The collecting is strong in this one...

Matt Fox tells us about his impressive collection

When were you first introduced to Star Wars toys?
I was five years old when I saw *Star Wars* in '77 and it also marked my first ever trip to a cinema – a double whammy on my young mind that soon became a triple whammy when the toys showed up at my local Woolworths, too. All I ever wanted for birthdays and Christmas were Star Wars toys, and I'd pore over the card backs and the product catalogues that showed the full figure line. On the reverse of each card back was the statement 'Collect them all', and I'm still trying to obey that simple command to this day!

When did you seriously start collecting Star Wars toys?
When the Special Edition returned to the cinema in 1997, it prompted me to rummage in my parents' loft and reclaim my old box of Star Wars toys. When I opened that box, I was hit full-

force by the golden glow of nostalgia – it was like the scene from *Pulp Fiction* when they look in the case! I had seen the light, and I really became an 'adult collector' from that moment on.

What's the crown jewel of your collection and why?
One of the very earliest items released in the vintage toy line was an 'action display stand' – a slick-looking gray stand with 12 foot pegs for the first 12 figures to proudly stand upon. This was reissued three years later to accompany *The Empire Strikes Back*, now in a new blood red box, with the iconic ESB logo, and most crucially containing six figures sealed in individual baggies. This reissued stand is beyond rare, with seemingly fewer than ten known to exist. I'm very proud to have one in my collection.

Tell us a little about your exhibition, May The Toys Be With You?
May The Toys Be With You is a collection of vintage Star Wars toys

and original movie posters. It's a beautifully presented and curated sci-fi exhibition that is touring museums around the UK. It's powerful nostalgia for those who lived through that era, but also really exciting and visual for new and young Star Wars fans too. The movie poster collection is particularly definitive.

What advice would you give to anyone who is interested in starting their own collection?
Best advice I ever heard was 'treat collecting as a marathon, not a sprint'. It doesn't even have to be expensive. I'd suggest starting with a loose figure collection. Once you've scored your toys, clean them with hot water and a soft brush, and you'll always end up with at least a few nice-condition complete ones. The rest you resell to pay for the ones you've kept.

Search for @maythetoysbewithyou on Facebook for all the latest updates on the exhibition.

MEDIA

Although there were only three core films, the hunger for Star Wars was strong. We examine how it expanded beyond the original trilogy

While the Star Wars toy line was incredibly successful for George Lucas, it wasn't a great way to expand the mythology of his beloved universe. Instead, the fertile franchise has grown through a variety of different mediums.

Comics and novels were the earliest such spin-offs. While the serialized story *The Keeper's World* ran in Marvel's *Pizzazz* comic in October 1977, the 1978 novel *Splinter Of The Mind's Eye* is generally considered to be the starting point for the 'Expanded Universe'. Featuring Luke Skywalker and Princess Leia, it had originally been intended as a low-budget sequel to *Star Wars* in case the original movie flopped. As Harrison Ford hadn't been signed on for any sequels at the time of writing, Han Solo didn't appear in it.

In 1987 West End Games released Star Wars: The Roleplaying Game, which offered further details about the many planets, races and vehicles found within the universe. It has continually evolved, even after West End Games lost the licence in 1998.

A series of comics by Dark Horse began in 1991 with *Dark Empire*, set six years after the end of *Return Of The Jedi*. Dark Horse continued to expand the universe until 2014, when comics moved to Disney-owned Marvel.

For many, the highlight of the Expanded Universe was the release of Timothy Zahn's *The Thrawn Trilogy*, which began in 1991 with *Heir To The Empire*. George Lucas had declared that many topics in the Star Wars universe, including the personal life of Anakin Skywalker and the rise of the Galactic Empire, were off-limits, so much of the Expanded Universe took place after Return Of The Jedi. It was Zahn's *Thrawn Trilogy* that was largely responsible for introducing a number of popular new characters, including Mara Jade, Grand Admiral Thrawn and the fleshing out of the

Many consider Timothy Zahn's *Thrawn* trilogy to be instrumental in helping to generate interest in Star Wars again.

Novels like *Vector Prime* greatly expanded *Star Wars'* lore but weren't always popular with fans.

Splinter Of The Mind's Eye was originally going to be a low-budget sequel to Star Wars.

Games like Dark Forces not only introduced new characters but also gave good insight into the back stories of existing ones.

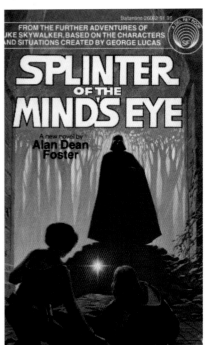

Imperial capital Coruscant, which would later feature prominently in the second Star Wars trilogy. Novels continued to shape and mould the Star Wars universe, but not all the choices made were popular with fans. Famed author RA Salvatore received death threats when he penned the novel *The New Jedi Order: Vector Prime*, which featured the death of Chewbacca, while others began to despair that there was so much contradiction between the Exapnded Universe and the films it was based on.

The Nineties was also an important time for Star Wars videogames. While they had existed since the early Eighties, it wasn't until the early Nineties that the capabilities of home computers and consoles were good enough for Lucasfilm to start expanding the Star Wars universe through the exciting new medium. Games like the *Dark Forces | Jedi Knight* series would introduce fans to important new characters like Kyle Katarn, while the likes of *Rogue Squadron* and the *X-Wing* series allowed you to relive some of the franchise's most exciting missions, as well as experience brand new ones. Games like *Shadow Of The Empire* typically featured brand new characters, as developers felt that it gave them more freedom while creating their games. They would also mine lesser characters from the films, fleshing them out in a way that the movies simply couldn't afford to do.

On 25 April 2014 Lucasfilm announced that the Expanded Universe would be retconned to take the new planned trilogy into account. As a result, all earlier non-film mentions of George Lucas's world would be placed under the Star Wars Legends banner and wouldn't be considered canon. While the news disgruntled some, Lucasfilm won't leave those characters out in the cold forever.

"The Thrawn Trilogy was responsible for introducing a number of popular new characters"

65

CONNECT 4

Connect 4 had Seventies kids well and truly gripped. The disc-dropping phenomenon had originated in the USA, where it was designed by renowned independent toy designer Ned Strongin, with Dr Howard Wexler, a City College graduate with a PhD in psychology.

But even though it has since been claimed to be a riff on a game called Captain's Mistress, which dates back to the days of explorer Captain Cook (while seemingly owing much to Tic Tac Toe), Connect 4 got its mass-market name because the idea was to become the first to get four discs in a row, whether horizontally, vertically or diagonally.

Winning a game should have been easy, but it wasn't. Playing on a vertical grid made up of seven columns and six rows, the advantage was always with the first player. Yet during the to-ing and fro-ing of this turn-based gem, players would seek to frustrate and outwit their opponent by thinking ahead. It was this degree of complexity that saw it fly off shop shelves following its 1974 debut. It was introduced in the UK two years later.

For those wondering, the key to winning was to pop the first disc into the center column since, in a game played perfectly from that point on, the opponent would always lose within 41 moves. That, however, assumed you had developed a knack for the game. With 42 pieces to place, and taking into account starting from zero, a Connect 4 board actually has a staggering 4,531,985,219,092 possible positions.

Information

Manufacturer: Milton Bradley
First Released: 1974
Expect to pay: $4

Connect 4 is all about offence and defence – aiming to bamboozle your opponent while trying to stop them getting four discs in a row. Decent players seek to put opponents in a pickle by ensuring their discs are so well positioned that they're able to win in one of two ways.

MB GAMES

Connect 4

The vertical strategy game

6-Adult
2 players

The writer and broadcaster Stuart Maconie was working on the music paper NME when he claimed David Bowie had invented Connect 4. He told the BBC that he had heard "people in pubs" tell him it was true. Unfortunately, as good as the story sounds, it was very much untrue.

UK catalogue retailer Argos sold Connect 4 for $3.79, a discount on the recommended price of $4.99. In today's prices that would be $21, which is roughly twice the price the current version by Hasbro would now set you back. That said, some argue the quality doesn't feel as robust as it did in the 1970s.

After assembling the plastic parts, players would choose a color and receive 21 discs. Each opponent then took it in turn to place a disc into one of the columns of the vertically stacked grid in a bid to get four in a row. Manufacturer Milton Bradley now suggests trying to win 10 games to be crowned a Connect 4 champion.

THE LEGACY

As well as coming in a multitude of sizes, including Giant Connect 4 that can be played outside of the home, the game and its underlying concept has also been turned into a series of videogames. There have been fresh variations too, including a 3D version for up to four players called Connect 4x4 and another called Connect 4 Twist & Turn, which is based around a tower made up of five twisting layers. On top of that are a host of clones.

SKATEBOARDS

All it took was a new set of wheels for skateboarding to roll its way back into the affection of the Seventies' youth

How it began

When Californian surfers began to attach roller skate wheels to wooden boards in the Fifties, everyone believed that the resulting phenomenon known as skateboarding would be around forever. It certainly appeared that way, especially between 1963 and 1965 when the sport was at its peak. But come 1970 and skateboarding in mainstream America had become about as fashionable as 'The Twist' in a local disco.

Had it not been for the entrepreneurial spirit of a young, pioneering surfer called Frank Nasworthy, then the likelihood is it would have remained that way. Instead, fate worked in skateboarding's favor and, on a visit to a friend's father's plastics factory called Creative Urethane in Purcellville, Virginia, Nasworthy made a startling discovery that would dramatically turn its fortunes around.

The factory was making wheels made of soft polyurethane, selling them to a firm called Roller Sports for use with rental skates at roller rinks. Nasworthy learned that the wheels lent greater traction and allowed for a smoother ride, and he believed that they would be the ideal replacements for the steel or clay wheels that had adorned skateboards since their invention.

As it turned out, this proved to be the case and Nasworthy successfully experimented with his own board. But it was only when he realized that pockets of hardcore surfers were still skateboarding on the Californian coast that he was able to put a plan into action. He struck a deal with Creative Urethane and set up the Cadillac Wheels Company in 1972. Yet in trying to sell the idea to surf shops in San Diego County, he came up against a wall of skepticism.

The biggest problem was that the wheels were slower than steel or clay so Nasworthy, who had invested $700 in his venture, had to work on making a breakthrough. He did this in 1973 by giving the wheels away for free, accompanied by a demonstration. Word soon got around. Those who tried the wheels loved the stability they brought and the way they could overcome small obstacles so that the skateboard would not come to a halt or skid.

As a result, within a month or so, the path for skateboarding's return to wider popularity was laid and Nasworthy's company went on to sell hundreds of thousands of wheels each and every year. What's more, the idea revolutionized not only the way the boards were created, but the entire art of skateboarding itself.

Going global

Encouraged by the newfound interest in the sport and the increased gripability of the wheels on concrete and roads, many manufacturers woke up to the possibilities. New decks began being made using fiberglass and aluminium, as well as wood, and they ranged from 50 to 120 centimeters in length.

"New tricks continued to be invented almost every day, as the action switched from natural urban settings to purpose-built skate parks complete with kickers and vertical ramps"

ESSENTIAL MERCH!

Z-Flex

After the Z-Boys, including Jay Adams, had established themselves in the skateboarding scene, they became involved in producing a new kind of skateboard. To do this they formed EZ-Ryder Skateboards, which became Z-Flex, and they pioneered the use of a concave on the board's topside while producing a smoother wheel.

Wes Humpston

If you can get hold of a Wes Humpston-designed skateboard, you'll be holding a true piece of history. As the original artist to design DogTown Skates, his artwork adorned the bottom of his skateboards and it grew in sophistication. Such was his influence that by the 1980s, such artwork was expected.

Powell Peralta

Founded by aerospace engineer George Powell and pro-skater Stacy Peralta in Santa Barbara, California, in 1978, Powell Peralta had a huge impact on the skateboarding scene and it ran its own skate team called Bones Brigade. It bridged the gap from the 1970s to the 1980s and made stars of skaters such as Tony Hawk.

But while it appeared that everyone wanted a slice of the action (skateboards were being used by postmen and factory workers among many others), scores of young people also wanted models with kicktails (an upward curve at the back). This widened the scope of what could be achieved on a skateboard in the name of fun and soon people were performing jumps, flips, spins, 360s, and even daffies, which made use of two skateboards, one in front of the other.

New tricks continued to be invented almost every day as the action switched from natural urban settings – many of which were described in the newly revived *Skateboarder* magazine from 1975 – to purpose-built skate parks complete with kickers and vertical ramps. These would have gentle beginner-friendly slopes as well as huge bowled areas that rose high into the air, enabling skateboarding to mimic surfing, and drawing in people more used to the sea.

A key moment came in the spring of 1975, however, when a team called Zephyr made up of soon-to-be big names such as Jay Adams, Stacy Peralta and Tony Alva caused jaws to drop with a new way of skateboarding. They appeared at a slalom and freestyling contest at the Ocean Festival in Del Mar, California, and showcased a style that would have the boarders lowering their bodies and smoothly performing hard turns. This really caught the imagination and soon more and more people wanted to give it a go.

This was also the case in 1978 when Alan Gelfand birthed street skateboarding by producing a move that became known as an ollie. It involved hitting the tail of the board and jumping, sending himself and the board into the air. With experiments also being carried out by manufacturers looking at different shapes and coming up with ever wider boards, skateboarding suddenly appeared edgy and cool. It was also a serious business: a custom-made high speed Ermico skateboard, for example, could cost about $2,000.

Not that skateboarding didn't have its downsides. In 1974 in America alone, 3,230 children aged five to 14 were treated in hospital following a skateboard accident and that shot up to 27,522 in 1975 and 71,438 in 1976, according to the *New York Times*. Only bikes and roller skates appeared to be involved in more accidents, with lower arms contusions and abrasions high on the list of ailments.

BAHNE
Precision Made Professional Skateboard Equipment

Love, laughter, good guys, bad guys and America's greatest skateboarders.

MOST DESIRABLE!
Bahne skateboards

Bahne was a big name in skateboarding throughout the 1970s, having evolved from making surfboards in the previous decade. The company was run by brothers Bill and Bob and it went on to form a close partnership with Frank Nasworthy's Cadillac Wheels, which put it at the forefront of the revitalized scene. At its height, Bahne was making a staggering thousand decks each day and it did so for three years. It also put its name to the infamous skateboard contest in Del Mar in 1975. Getting hold of any vintage Bahne skateboard, then, will be a cool addition to anyone's collection given the history it represents.

Such accidents caused skateboarding to fade again in the early Eighties as insurance premiums at skate parks rose. By this point, however, it had already attracted fans and a new breed of collectors. Some of the key skateboard makers had innovated with improved ball bearings and specially designed trucks for sport, so people were increasingly keen to get their hands on them.

Logan Earth Ski, for instance, produced solid wooden decks of the highest quality that would set you back around $50 today for an unprinted model. The company's decks were also popular with some of the major stars, among them Tony Alva, and it was a leader in the urethane revolution.

But it was far from the only one. Gordon & Smith, which had become a major manufacturer of surfboards in the Sixties, grew to become one of the most successful skateboard companies and among the first to sponsor pro riders. Its Fiberflex skateboards had a six-month waiting list and it was known for its cutting edge wood and fiberglass laminates.

Since many skateboarders took to empty swimming pools – taking advantage of the Californian drought

between 1976 and 1978 that forced owners to drain them – Gordon & Smith produced a popular model called the Stacey Peralta Warp Tail with Roadrider 4 wheels and Bennett trucks that would enable them to pull off neat tricks. Santa Cruz Skateboards, meanwhile, used top-of-the-range Sims Pure Juice Rider Wheels for better control. Others had the coolest of art.

All aboard
Wes Humpston was a pioneer of skateboard art and the man behind the original raw and territorial Dogtown designs of the late Seventies. The Dogtown cross was a powerful symbol and it came to reflect a particular strand of American youth culture.

This also transcended well in the UK where another important scene had grown, having rolled over from California. British kids lapped up the lingo and they'd be heard talking of "eating it", "street pizza" and "road rash" to describe particular types of falls. They'd become "stoked" at the mere thought of riding.

British kids ahead of the curve would import their boards, but UK manufacturers soon got in on the

act with their own models, costing around $7. Just as in America, the Royal Society for the Prevention of Accidents warned against riding on the streets and open roads and there were fears, expressed in *The Observer* newspaper in 1977, that as many as 4,300 British children could be hospitalized each year.

That didn't happen and skateboarding has had resurgences since, particularly in the 1990s and 2000s. A good number also try their hand at the sport from the safe distance of videogames such as the *Tony Hawk* and *Skate* series, but they're just not the same. You can't get the same thrill of pirouetting through the air with a games controller in your hand, no matter how stoked you may be.

SPEAK & SPELL

Information

Manufacturer: Texas Instruments
First Released: 1978
Expect to pay: $299.99 (for original model)

Is it too dramatic to call Speak & Spell the iPad of the Seventies? Almost certainly, but there's no denying that the two have at least one thing in common. Using a Speak & Spell felt as though you were holding and playing with cutting-edge technology, even if Speak & Spell was very much a toy.

Speak & Spell was actually an educational toy, and even though child logic often dictated that education isn't fun, this bright orange device overcame the label by dazzling users with its tech. It was designed to help children pronounce and spell words correctly – hence 'Speak & Spell' – and it was the wonder of hearing the device actually speak rather than play back a pre-recorded voice that ensured it didn't feel dull or boring. It made young minds wonder what sort of technological sorcery was taking place under the bright casing, and its spell-binding magic is what earned it a place in childhood legend.

What helped was that Speak & Spell had lots of word games, too. The basic unit had Mystery Word, Secret Code, and Letter. Additional cartridge expansions, in what would serve as a sort of precursor of things to come with handheld consoles like the Game Boy, contained further games such as A.C.E. and Race. At the height of its popularity, Speak & Spell wasn't just helping to educate children – it even enabled a certain alien to phone home in Steven Spielberg's film *E.T.*

Speak & Spell was actually part of a three-toy launch. Texas Instruments also launched *Speak & Read* and *Speak & Math* alongside it, although they never reached the same heights that *Speak & Spell* did.

The synthesized speech is so popular that it has actually crossed over into music. It has been sampled by bands like Coldplay, Limp Bizkit and TLC, while Depeche Mode's *Speak & Spell* album was named after the device.

Speak & Spell was created when Texas Instruments begun work on speech synthesis, with its $25,000 research into the area eventually leading to the creation of the educational toy. It was the first educational toy to use speech that wasn't pre-recorded on tape.

THE LEGACY

While Speak & Spell helped influence the educational development of many young lives, its lasting impact was in the technology used. By synthesizing a spoken word rather than playing back a voice recording, Speak & Spell paved the way for technology used in devices today such as Siri. Online emulators mean Speak & Spell fans can easily relive memories on their desktops, rather than hunting down an original model through eBay.

HELLO_

TEXAS INSTRUMENTS

One of the features that helped Speak & Spell endure was its compatibility with 'expansion modules', cartridges that could be purchased separately that added new words and games. These could be inserted through the battery slot.

OFF GO REPLAY REPEAT CLUE MYSTERY WORD SECRET CODE LETTER SAY IT SPELL

A B C D E F G H I J
K L M N O P Q R S T
U V W X Y Z

© TI 1978

MODULE SELECT   ERASE   ENTER

Speak & Spell™

During the late 1990s, The Ohio Art Company was in financial trouble even though it had sold more than 100 million units by 1999. Luckily, John Lasseter, the director of *Toy Story 2*, wanted to incorporate the toy into his movie. With an estimated $50 million worth of free advertising, sales boomed by 20 percent.

THE LEGACY

The Etch A Sketch has remained a popular purchase for most of the past 50 years and there have been numerous attempts to keep it fresh. The Animator was released in the 1980s, for instance, incorporating a low-res dot matrix display, while a color version was launched in 1993. Today, it's possible to buy Etch A Sketch mobile apps, plus a scene of dedicated artists has grown around the device, each of whom are producing the most astounding lineographic artwork.

Information

Manufacturer: The Ohio Art Company
First Released: 1960
Expect to pay: $15

The Ohio Art Company had originally spotted L'Écran Magique at an International Toy Fair in Nuremberg, Germany, in 1959. It decided to pass on the idea, however, only picking it up later when it saw the idea again and felt it could be a huge hit. It was released in time for Christmas 1960.

MAGIC Etch A Sketch SC

Gagliardi

Etch A Sketch MAG

THE AMAZING

unlimited design possibi

SKE

ANOT

THE AMAZING

Etch A Sketch

MAGIC SCREEN

PRINT! Write! DRAW!

HOURS OF *fascinating* FUN FOR THE ENTIRE FAMILY

turn face down and shake to erase

ETCH A SKETCH

E ven though it was arguably less versatile than pen and paper, there was something rather charming about the simple-looking Etch A Sketch. Popular during the 1970s, it presented kids with a blank canvas that was crying out for input. Indeed, few could resist fiddling with the knobs, even if most of us ended up drawing simple stuff like houses, flowers and the crudest of faces.

Many of us knew that one kid, of course, who would create jaw-dropping images that would have truly amazed the playground, if only the plastic drawing toy had not jiggled around so much in their bag. But that was the beauty of André Cassagnes' invention: it could unleash creativity on the most basic of levels and yet promise so much more.

Cassagnes was a French electrician and, in 1955, he had noted how an electrostatic charge was able to cling aluminium to glass. It prompted him to develop L'Écran Magique, or The Magic Screen, which was eventually picked up by The Ohio Art Company for $25,000 and handed to chief engineer Jerry Burger to help perfect for the masses.

Key to the toy was a fine aluminium powder mixed with tiny polystirene beads that allowed for even distribution. A stylus operated by two knobs could then be moved vertically and horizontally, scraping the aluminium from the screen to create black lines.

In doing so, artworks sprang from the screen before being erased by shaking the toy so that the powder would resettle. Such was its attraction that it sold in its millions, with Ohio Art launching "cool blue" and "hot pink" versions alongside the traditional red framed version during the 1970s.

Among those who have proven rather proficient at creating Etch A Sketch drawings is Jeff Gagliardi, of Boulder, Colorado, who takes between five and 20 hours to produce his amazing artwork using nothing but the toy. But while he picked up the skill as an art student in the Schools of Visuals Arts in New York City in the 1970s, he never actually had one as a child.

The reason the lines are black is because the interior of the Etch A Sketch itself is dark. The background is only revealed to the user when the aluminium powder is moved away by the built-in stylus, allowing for the stark contrast with the light gray of the rest of the screen.

TOP SHOWS

FROM THE SEVENTIES

An era of gritty realism, social struggles and gentle kid. shows kept us glued to our color television.

One of the most important changes for television in the 1970s was the mass adoption of color TV sets. By the turn of the decade, channels had begun regularly broadcasting their programs in color, having started to experiment in 1967. As a consequence, there were 1.6 million color sets in 1972 and the number of color TV licences soared to some 12 million soon after.

To encourage more people to switch and to take advantage of this important evolution, broadcasters started to rethink how they made their shows. For them, color was an opportunity to deliver greater realism, so the 1970s not only saw pictures that better represented real life, they also benefited from a plethora of gritty dramas that sought to absorb viewers like never before.

At the same time, people were becoming more aspirational, with an increasing number defining themselves as middle class. This was best reflected in the tone of sitcoms, which typically highlighted and poked fun at the shift. American television was also becoming more socially conscious, while shedding past genres such as westerns. It looked to ape cinema, too, with fast-paced action dramas and movies made for TV. Television, it seems, was coming of age.

Scooby-Doo, Where Are You!

1969–1970

2 For many of us, our Saturday mornings started with Fred, Daphne, Velma, Shaggy, and their talking dog, Scooby-Doo, as they solved supernatural mysteries and caught bad guys red-handed. Created by Joe Ruby and Ken Spears in 1969, *Scooby-Doo, Where Are You!* was intended to appease parents by not abiding to the popular, and violent, superhero format. The funny rag-tag group of teens called Mystery Incorporated quickly won the hearts of parents and kids alike. And although spooky at times, the program proved successful, making it one of the biggest franchises in history. The original series only aired from 1969–1970 but led to a plethora of new media in the following years.

Schoolhouse Rock!

1973–1985

1 When David McCall, an executive of McCaffrey and McCall, discovered that his son struggled to learn multiplication tables, he hired musician Bob Dorough to write a song to help his son remember. The song was called "Three Is a Magic Number" and inspired illustrator Tom Yohe, who worked for the same company as McCall, to create visuals for the catchy tune. It was later pitched to ABC as a television series and debuted on-screen in January 1973. *Schoolhouse Rock!* named its first season "Multiplication Rock," which combined music and math to create easy-to-understand 3-minute videos for young audiences. It was the longest-running educational short on ABC, lasting from 1973–1985, because of its massive success and popularity. *Schoolhouse Rock's* memorable sound still exists in the minds of Americans today, with the most famous jingle being "Conjunction Junction, What's Your Function?" from the "Grammar Rock" season.

The Brady Bunch

1969–1974

3 When widowed Mike Brady married single mother Carol Martin, they were also marrying their families, which consisted of three sons and three daughters, resulting in America's most famous blended family. *The Brady Bunch* was created by Sherwood Schwartz and aired from 1969–1974 but was not an initial success during its original run. However, after syndication in 1975, the program became a staple in homes across America. *The Brady Bunch* focused on lighthearted themes such as household dynamic, teen and preteen drama, responsibility, self-image, sibling rivalry, character building, and more. It also omitted any political commentary, allowing viewers an escape from the political commotion of the Vietnam War at the time.

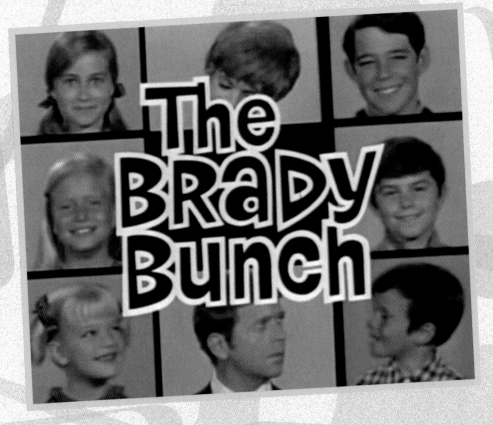

The Six Million Dollar Man

1973–1978

4 The best ideas always get revived, which is why a movie based on this iconic sci-fi TV series is in production (as the Six Billion Dollar Man). The original saw Lee Majors play a former astronaut called Colonel Steve Austin who gained superhero strength thanks to expensive bionic implants. Employed as a secret agent by the US government, viewers enjoyed both the stories and the cool method of storytelling, which included slow-motion action and electronic sound effects. Inspired by the cult novel Cyborg by Martin Caidin, it also transcended the screen thanks to a popular range of accompanying toys.

Taxi

1978–1983

5 Centered around the unsatisfied employees of the Sunshine Cab Company, *Taxi* combines comradery and companionship as cabbies form unlikely friendships and help each other through life's obstacles. The premise of the show was inspired by a nonfiction article featured in New York Magazine about night shift cab drivers working for a New York cab company. The idea for a television series about cab drivers was sparked by James L. Brooks and David Davis, though the article was never referenced during development. This award-winning sitcom aired on ABC from 1978–1982 and on NBC from 1982–1983, gathering massive success during each of its runs. The brilliant ensemble cast, unique character backgrounds and dynamics, real-life themes, and overall comedic aspect launched *Taxi* to its fame.

Good Times

1974

6 You may recognize the two starring leads of this sitcom from another popular sitcom called *Maude*, which was a spin-off of *All in the Family*. Main characters Florida and her husband James (renamed from Henry) were small roles in *Maude*, but they were likable enough to get their own series. Created by Eric Monte and Mike Evans in 1974, *Good Times* aimed to offer a broader glimpse into the lives of black Americans living in housing projects in Chicago, thus becoming the first two-parent African American family sitcom. It tackled the themes of overcoming poverty, living in public housing, working multiple odd jobs, and dealing with everyday hurdles and concerns. Florida, James, and their three children stole the hearts of Americans and ran for six long seasons, with their son J.J. gaining the most popularity because of his famous phrase, "Dy-no-mite!"

Land of the Lost

1974–1976

7 A live action, kid-friendly, family adventure series in an alternate universe with cave people, humanoid lizard species, daunting dinosaurs, and a killer theme song. What could be better? Producers Sid and Marty Krofft were ambitious in their attempt at stop-motion animation for the dinosaurs and lizard creatures, and their great effort landed them success and popularity with viewers of all ages. The show follows the Marshall family, Rick, Holly, and Will, as they try to survive their new reality and find a way back home. They encounter exotic creatures, friendly inhabitants, and a dangerous species known as Sleestak. *Land of the Lost* aired on Saturday mornings on NBC from 1974–1976 and is now considered a 70s cult classic. It has since been remade in the 90s as a series and again in 2009 as a hit comedy film, starring Will Ferrell.

The Tom and Jerry Show

1975

8 First created in 1940, Tom and Jerry had already won the hearts of millions when the first spin-off was made. *The Tom and Jerry Show* only aired for 16 three-segment episodes in 1975 as the first part of *The Great Grape Ape Show* and *The Mumbly Cartoon Show*. Rather than have the classic slapstick chases and violent encounters between Tom and Jerry, this mini-series features the cat and mouse duo working together on various adventures. Despite not abiding to the original *Tom and Jerry* feud, kids still tuned in to *The Tom and Jerry Show* on Saturday mornings. In fact, many versions of *Tom and Jerry* are continually rerun on television today.

I, Claudius

1976

10 Based on the 1934 novel by the English writer Robert Graves, this historical BBC drama series was a gripping retrospective look at the life of the Roman Emperor Claudius. Filmed in a studio for artistic reasons and starring a host of great actors including Derek Jacobi, Siân Phillips and a young Brian Blessed, it felt claustrophobic and moved at a slow pace. But it covered a tumultous and violent period that allowed the writers to cut through numerous taboos and, while critics initially panned it, they were soon won around. What's more, having won numerous awards, it went on to inspire the making of the 1980s US show *Dynasty*.

Kojak

1973–1978

9 Perhaps one of the most iconic characters of American television is detective lieutenant Theodopolis "Theo" Kojak. Tough, honest, witty, and dapper, lieutenant Kojak was always styling sunglasses with a lollipop in his mouth, uttering his most famous catchphrase, "Who loves ya, baby?" Kojak spends his days fighting crime for the New York City Police Department, even if it means bending the rules. Airing from 1973–1978, *Kojak* was created by Abby Mann to highlight the themes of civil injustice and institutionalized prejudice. Its raw, intense, dramatic portrayal of the inner workings of New York's finest caught the attention of viewers across the nation, causing it to soar in popularity.

The Odd Couple

1970–1975

11 divorced sportswriter and his newly separated best friend move in together in Manhattan, New York. While their dynamic as friends is strong, their life together proves difficult due to their opposite personalities. One is neat, one is messy, one is logical, one is emotional, and both are determined to be right. Based on the 1965 play written by Neil Simon, *The Odd Couple* aired from 1970–1975 on ABC and quickly gained devoted viewers because of the hilarious, dysfunctional relationship between Oscar and Felix. The series proved widely successful, even years after its end, with two episodes landing spots on TV Guide's 100 Greatest Episodes of All Time in 1997: "Password" at number 5 and "The Fat Farm" at number 58.

Emergency!

1972–1977

12 During a time when ambulance coverage and the paramedic profession were gaining popularity in American society, *Emergency!* centered around a paramedic-firefighter duo who formed a medical rescue unit in the Los Angeles County Fire Department called Squad 51. The rescuers, Johnny Gage and Roy DeSoto, work with the medical staff of the fictional hospital, Rampart General, and Station 51 of the firefighter engine company. *Emergency!* gained nation-wide attention because it portrayed the realistic yet gripping ins and outs of the medical field in the Los Angeles metropolitan area. Created by Robert Cinader and Jack Webb, the series ran for six seasons from 1972–1977, and had six more two-hour films in 1978 and 1979. After an iconic run, the show landed a spot in the Smithsonian's National Museum of American History where much of the show's memorabilia sits on display.

CHiPs

1977–1983

13 This action-packed crime drama focuses on Officer Francis "Ponch" Poncherello and his partner, Officer Jonathan "Jon" Baker, as they tackle fast-paced pursuits on California highways. Ponch and Jon are both motorcycle officers who work for the California Highway Patrol (CHP), hence the name *CHiPs*. Although they work as a pair, Ponch and Jon fight crime in vastly different ways, with Jon taking the diligent approach and Ponch seizing any moment for a troublesome shortcut. *CHiPs* was created by Rick Rosner, who aimed at portraying a comedic yet thrilling series. Luckily for Rosner, crime dramas were all the rage during its run from 1977–1983, making *CHiPs* an immediate hit with audiences.

Starsky And Hutch

1975–1979

14 Influenced by the decade's gritty police movies – in particular *Dirty Harry* – the small-screen partnership of undercover detectives Dave Starsky and Ken Hutchinson not only made for compulsive viewing in the latter part of the 1970s, but helped to develop the now-familiar buddy cop dynamic. It mirrored the movies with its numerous shoot-outs and frenetic car chases while ticking every box for the genre, from the handsome polar opposite leads and gorgeous women to the glamorous Californian setting and jive-talking informant Huggy Bear. It even had a cool red Ford Gran Turismo with a white stripe down its side. What's not to love?

Dukes of Hazzard

1979–1985

15 One of the most popular action comedies of the 70s was *The Dukes of Hazzard*, which was consistently on the top-rated list of television series at the time of its air, from 1979–1985. It was adapted from the 1975 film *Moonrunners* by Gy Waldron and turned into a family-friendly actions series. Main characters Bo and Luke Duke are cousins who are on probation for illegally running moonshine. The Duke boys live in Hazzard County, Georgia, where they always get caught in the middle of daring adventures and small-town conflicts. Each episode follows them as they dodge the corrupt county commissioner and probation officer, Boss Hogg, and race around in their bright orange 1969 Dodge Charger, nicknamed The General Lee. Despite being made out to be the county troublemakers, the Dukes often convey their good nature by helping others, even Boss Hogg and other adversaries.

Dallas

1978–1991

16 Still existing as one of the longest lasting prime time drama series in American television history, *Dallas* aired from 1978–1991 with a whopping 357 episodes. This soap opera focuses on the Ewings, a prominent Texas family who owns an oil company and cattle ranch. The original tension in the series was built around the marriage of Bobby Ewing and Pamela Barnes, who come from archrival families. However, a majority of the show's drama stems from Bobby's brother, J.R. Ewing, a money-hungry oil tycoon who is constantly formulating schemes to get ahead of his brother. *Dallas*'s incredible ensemble cast and riveting themes of wealth, conflict, intrigue, sex, and power struggles kept fans interested for as long as it aired. The show was also well-known for its nail-biting cliffhangers, leaving audiences yearning for new episodes each week. *Dallas* made such an impact on television that it landed a spot on Time Magazine's list of 100 Best TV Shows of All-Time in 2007.

Fantasy Island

1977–1984

17 A fantasy drama series that aired from 1977–1984, Fantasy Island was created by Gene Levitt and starred Ricardo Mantalbán, who played Mr. Roarke, and Hervé Villechaize, who played his assistant named Tattoo. For a price, guests to the mysterious island— that was located somewhere in the Atlantic Ocean off the coast of French Guiana— could come and live out their fantasies. There were 7 seasons of the show, resulting in 152 episodes. In 1998, a one-season revival aired, followed by a horror prequel movie in 2020 (that ultimately flopped review-wise) and a TV series reboot in 2021. Before the original TV show aired, it was first introduced to viewers as two made-for-TV films.

Mork & Mindy

1978–1982

18 Robin Williams' Mork made his first appearance in *Happy Days* season five episode *My Favorite Orkan* ("nanu nanu"). At that time the actor was doing the rounds as a stand-up comedian, but the extra-terrestrial made such an impression that producer Garry Marshall created a spin-off sitcom, bringing on board Pam Dawber as his human roommate Mindy. The show's wholesome nature and the pair's adorable relationship hooked as many as 60 million viewers at its peak, with Williams drawing on his comedy background by seemingly ad-libbing his way through scenes. The comedy also had to use four cameras to keep up with Williams' frenetic movements.

M*A*S*H

1972–1983

19 Spawned from the 1970 movie, which in turn was adapted from a 1968 novel, the dark American war comedy *M*A*S*H* ran for an impressive 11 seasons. It was set during the Korean War of 1950 to 1953 and centered around the Mobile Army Surgical Hospital, hence the show's name. Yet it was first aired against the backdrop of the ongoing Vietnam War and so it was as much about capturing disillusionment with the current situation, making it as poignant as it was funny. Such was its popularity that the final episode drew the largest audience to date – given the strength of the acting and writing, it was not difficult to see why.

Charlie's Angels

1976–1981

20 Originally meant to be called *The Alley Cats*, *Charlie's Angels* evolved into a sassy crime drama about three women working in a LA private detective agency. The new title reflected the introduction of mysterious retired detective Charlie Townsend, who would give the women their missions. But, given he was never seen on screen, it became purely about girl power, making big stars of Jaclyn Smith, Kate Jackson and, of course, Farrah Fawcett. Of the three, Fawcett became a generation's pin-up thanks in no small part to her revealing clothing. Such was the strength of the show, however, it survived her leaving after the first series and remains cult viewing today.

The Muppet Show

1976–1981

21 When two pilot episodes of Jim Henson's latest creation failed to catch the attention of the US networks in 1974 and 1975, Lew Grade, the boss of ATV in the UK, made him an offer. It subsequently saw The Muppet Show made at Elstree, England, and it proved to be a shrewd move. By the third series, in 1978, the heavily syndicated show had become the most-watched on Earth as 235 million people became glued to the in-theater antics of Kermit the Frog, Fozzie Bear, Gonzo the Great and Miss Piggy. Its trick was to appeal to adults as much as kids, and legends were truly born.

Sanford And Son

1972–1977

22 Having seen the success of the BBC comedy *Steptoe And Son*, which had aired since 1962, the US network NBC snapped up a remade American version and saw it soar to the top of the ratings. Starring comedian Redd Fox as the junk dealer Fred Stanford and Demond Wilson as son Lamont Sanford, it was called out by the New York Times in 1973 as being a "white show" with black characters. But it was nevertheless one of the first primetime African-American TV shows that, amid the laughs, highlighted the prejudices and challenges being faced during the decade, and it rightly became a true classic.

The Waltons

1972–1981

23 With a dozen Emmys under its belt over a nine-season run, *The Waltons* was a hugely successful show about a family of seven children living in rural Virginia during the Depression. It stood out for refusing to equate success with violence or overt heroism, preferring instead to reflect a low-key life. Indeed, the main character, John Boy, was modeled on the show's creator, Earl Hamner Jr, and the familiar "Goodnight, John Boy" closing sequence was inspired by a bedtime routine in his own childhood home. Hamner would also briefly narrate each episode, informing viewers of his own time living in the Blue Ridge Mountains, making it a deeply personal show.

The Rockford Files

1974 –1980

25 This Emmy-winning TV drama series followed the misadventures of a wisecracking small-time ex-convict private eye called Jim Rockford, played by James Garner, who had previously risen to fame in the 1950s western *Maverick*. It brought the detective genre up to date and combined the production talents of Roy Huggins and Stephen J Cannell to create a series that looked to eschew the glamorous lifestyle then typically associated with detectives. Indeed, it had the lead character living and working in a mobile home, taking on the cases that few others wanted. He'd also look to avoid fights for fear of attracting the police, even though he'd still often get a pasting.

Happy Days

1974–1984

24 Before *Happy Days* "jumped the shark" in 1977 (a term that entered the lexicon after a water-skiing Fonzie leapt over a shark and stretched the show's credibility), this US sitcom rode high in viewer affections. Having originally focused on Richie Cunningham's adolescent life, it soon positioned Arthur 'the Fonz' Fonzarelli as the major star and not only did this change the direction of the show and make it instantly popular, it arguably changed the approach of many sitcoms. The acting was played up, the plots dumbed down and the laughs relentlessly pursued, but it shot to number one and nailed down character types that became staples of later comedies.

Columbo

1971–1978

26 *Columbo* turned the whodunnit genre on its head by identifying each episode's murderer in the opening minutes before following the disheveled police lieutenant's shrewd attempts to apprehend them. Today, it's hard to imagine anyone other than Peter Falk wearing the shabby beige raincoat (more so given it was the actor's own, bought during a New York rainstorm in 1967 for $15). But the role was originally offered to Bing Crosby, who turned it down, preferring games of golf to a character that would become iconic. Some of the killers included Patrick McGoohan (who starred as a murderer four times), George Hamilton and William Shatner. Oh, and one more thing: it won an Emmy in its first season.

Price is Right

...lay

Holding the record for longest-running game show of all time, *The Price is Right* has aired on American television for 58 years (over 9,000 episodes!), ...cludes its nine-year run from 1956–1965 before ...ramped in 1972 as the version we know now. This ...ting, interactive, family-friendly game show was an ...on for many game shows that proceeded it. The show ...nine randomly selected members of a live audience ...go through a sequence of challenges until there are ...lists who compete in the final challenge, known as the ...se, where they bid on prizes and the closest bid wins ...w. Bob Barker hosted *The Price is Right* from 1972 until ...rement in 2007 when current host Drew Carey took ...ou can catch Drew Carey's version of the show every ...ay on CBS at 11:00 a.m. if you're feeling nostalgic.

...l in the Family

...–1979

8 Narrow-minded family man Archie Bunker and his sweet but ditzy wife Edith live in Queens, New York. They're a traditional blue-collar working ...ly but their daughter, Gloria, is an ardent feminist, ...her husband, Michael, shares her progressive thoughts ...interests. The relationship between these two couples ...esents the aftermath of the counterculture of the 60s, ...n Baby Boomers clashed with the conventional beliefs ...he Greatest Generation. *All in the Family* was produced ...Norman Lear and Bud Yorkin and ran for nine seasons ...n 1971–1979. This series was amongst the first to focus on ...newhat taboo topics for television, like racism, infidelity, ...e, religion, abortion, cancer, antisemitism, homosexuality, ...minism, and more. By portraying many controversial ...bjects, *All in the Family* became one of the most influential ...coms of the time, and still remains one of the greatest ...evision shows in U.S. history. It topped the Nielsen ratings ...r five years in a row from 1971–1976, ranked number four ...TV Guide's 50 Greatest TV Shows of All Time, ranked ...urth again by the Writers Guild of America, and Bravo ...amed Archie Bunker the greatest TV character of all time.

The Jeffersons

1975–1985

29 Developed as a spin-off of *All in the Family*, *The Jeffersons* centers around the next-door neighbors of Archie and Edith Bunker. Louise, George, and their son Lionel move from Queens, New York to luxurious Manhattan because of George's successful dry-cleaning business. *The Jeffersons* highlights the rise in wealth of an African American family as they "move on up" the money ladder, which was much different than previous depictions of black Americans on television. It is a traditional sitcom but occasionally touches on serious topics such as racism, suicide, gun control, alcoholism, transgenderism, and more. The show proved a hit during its air from 1975–1985, making it one of the longest-running sitcoms in history. It is also the first show to feature an interracial couple as prominent characters. *The Jeffersons* was popular for its new on-screen perspective of the black community, making it influential in the world of television and beyond.

Wonder Woman

1975–1979

30 Starring the beautiful Lynda Carter as Diana Prince, *Wonder Woman* is a superhero series that became an instant hit with audiences due to its dazzling production and action-packed plot. It was developed from the DC comics and first made into a TV film, *The New Original Wonder Woman*, which also starred Carter. The film pilot was a tremendous success, leading to the production of the *Wonder Woman* series. Taking place during WWII, the show follows Diana, an Amazon princess, as she fights D.C. crime and eradicates Nazi enemies, often riding in her invisible plane and styling her iconic uniform. The pilot film aired in 1975 and was followed by the series in 1976. The show was on a ratings high for the first two seasons but dwindled in the third and final season. However, *Wonder Woman* remains a cult classic and has since been reproduced into a blockbuster movie in 2017 as part of the DC film universe, which Carter even cameoed in.

The Incredible Hulk

1978–1982

31 Before the Marvel Cinematic Universe became the formidable film franchise it is now, superhero and comic book lovers were able to indulge in the classic television series, *The Incredible Hulk*. Dr. David Banner lives with a secret that can put others in harms way. After a scientific alteration of his cells, Banner can transform into a 7-foot tall, 330-pound, green humanoid, dubbed "the Hulk," when he's stressed or angry. While the Hulk frequently stops crime with his super-strength, he is often fighting his own ferocious temper while trying not to hurt the people around him. The series aired from 1978–1982 for five seasons. It was widely popular with a variety of age groups and was steadily in the top 50 TV shows during its entire run. It even became a hit in Europe, where superhero shows were much less watched.

Little House on the Prairie

1974–1982

32 Amongst the sitcoms, crime dramas, and superhero action shows was a less thrilling but more endearing historical series. *Little House on the Prairie* was a far cry from the comedic and flamboyant shows at the time of its air, but still yielded the dramatic appeal that audiences longed for on their screens. The series was adapted from the best-selling *Little House* book series by Laura Ingalls Wilder and aired from 1974–1982 on NBC. Episodes centered on the Ingalls, a family of five, and their quaint life on a Minnesota farm, taking place in the late 1800s. Much of the shows commentary and drama touched on the themes of adoption, alcoholism, faith, poverty, prejudice, and more. The close-knit family dynamic of the Ingalls and their overall compassion kept viewers wanting more, making it a massive success. *Little House on the Prairie* produced three made-for-... as well as a miniseries adaption in 2005.

The Partridge Family

1970–1974

34 Airing from 1970–1974, *The Partridge Family* entertained audiences with their musical talents and family quarrels. In the pilot episode, the five children of widowed mother Shirley Partridge, played by Shirley Jones, convince her to sing while they perform a pop song in their garage. It doesn't take long for her determined son, Danny, played by David Cassidy, to find them a manager to go on tour. The series follows the Partridges as they tour to different musical venues in their iconic multicolored 1957 Chevrolet Series 6800 Superior, but most episodes take place in their suburban California home. The show was well received by critics and audiences alike, earning two nominations for Best TV Show – Musical/Comedy in 1971 and 1972. *The Partridge Family* franchise boomed, producing books, board games, apparel, and multiple albums. And although the whole family is seen singing and playing on-screen, only Cassidy and occasionally Jones are actually featured in the recordings.

Laverne & Shirley

1976–1982

33 Taking place in the late 50s, Laverne and Shirley, played by Penny Marshall and Cindy Williams, live together in Milwaukee, Wisconsin and work as bottle cappers at a local brewery. However, from the sixth season onward, the setting changes to mid-60s in Burbank, California. *Laverne & Shirley* is a spin-off of the popular sitcom *Happy Days*, where the girls were featured as acquaintances of Fonzie. The series follows them as they navigate their life as roommates and as two single women out on their own. *Laverne & Shirley* aired from 1976–1982 for eight seasons, bringing devoted fans along with it. According to Nielsen ratings, the third season was the most-watch American TV program in 1977. From the laugh-out-loud moments to the tender and compassionate friendships, comedic conquests, and incredible cast, *Laverne & Shirley* remains a classic favorite to this day.

Fawlty Towers

1975–1979

35 *Fawlty Towers* was initially turned down by the BBC in 1974, with Ian Main, the head of comedy and light entertainment, musing, "I thought this one as dire as its title." But contrary to that prediction, *Fawlty Towers* was packed with memorable lines and madcap situations as John Cleese's Basil Fawlty not only battled to make his Torquay hotel a success but fought against his bossy wife Sybil. Add cunning chambermaid Polly and the put-upon Spanish waiter Manuel and you had a comedy that poked fun at ignorance and inept management while also succeeding in satirizing upper-class bigotry. Physical stunts left Andrew Sachs beaten black and blue but, after just two series, it left audiences dearly wanting more.

SIMON

If you remember Simon, then chances are your memory is working more effectively than when you were actually playing this iconic, electronic game back in the day. Invented by Ralph H Baer and programmed by Lenny Cope, the pattern-forming plaything had people trying to recall and repeat a sequence of tones and lights. The more successful you were, the longer and more complex it got. It was nothing if not tough.

Shoehorned into 1K of memory and using a 4-bit processor, Simon was initially going to be a simple rectangular box. When it was licensed to Milton Bradley, however, Dorothy Wooster, the daughter-in-law of the company's president, insisted on some changes. In came three game variations, difficulty levels and additional switches. Meanwhile, an unsung hero changed the shape. As a result, Simon went on to sell a

million within months of being released.

There was something rather attractive and mesmerizing about the end product; a circular device with its red, green, blue and yellow coloring, and bugle-inspired notes. Gameplay may have been reduced to clicking the plastic buttons in the right order (the manual noted you shouldn't punch or jab them), but there was no doubt the game had depth.

The hardest skill level was four: for this, you needed to recall 31 sequences, way up on the eight required for the first level. Considering the tempo would increase after the fifth, ninth and 13th sequences, this was no mean feat, especially when you only had five seconds to recall and then repeat. After all, no one wanted to hear the "razz" sound of a loser: it was so much better when you were victorious.

▼

Simon made use of four tones and the aim was to make them harmonic regardless of the sequence. The blue button emitted an E and the yellow button played a C-sharp. Red was an A and green was an E that was an octave lower than the blue.

Information

Manufacturer: Milton Bradley
First Released: 1978
Expect to pay: $20

▲

Simon was inspired by a waist-high, screenless arcade machine called Touch Me, which had four buttons and tasked people with following random sequences. It had been released by Atari in 1974 but only when Simon brought the concept to the home did Atari follow suit by releasing a handheld version of its own.

THE LEGACY

Following the release of the original, Milton Bradley created a smaller version called Pocket Simon and it also produced an eight-button device named Super Simon. Over the years, further alterations have been made. History has seen the release of hexagonal Simons, extra game modes and a version based on drumsticks. The latest version, Simon Optix, is a wearable headset that beams random sequences of lights into your eyes (and sounds into your ears) before getting you to move your hands in the correct order.

The game went through a series of names before it was finally called Simon. They included Follow-Me, Tap-Me and Feedback. Simon was chosen because the gameplay was similar to the children's game Simon Says. When it made its debut in the USA, it cost American consumers $24.95.

5 WAYS TO PLAY
For fast and furious play action, see back.

OMPUTER CONTROLLED GAME

Simon

K FAST! Simon says repeat my flashing LIGHTS and SOUNDS

The device made its debut on 15 May 1978 in an unusual setting: the 1970s hotspot, Studio 54, in New York City. Despite only being open for 33 months, it had become the world's most famous nightclub, so Milton Bradley's flamboyant VP George Ditomassi had a four-foot version of the game float above the heads of revelers at 2am as a promotional stunt.

BREYER HORSES

Information

Manufacturer: Breyer Animal Creations
First Released: 1950
Expect to pay: $30-80

More than a few companies have stumbled upon their most famous product by accident. In 1950, Breyer was reeling from the loss of a government contract to produce custom-molded plastic products when the decorative element produced for a clock helped the company find new life. The decorative element was a plastic horse and Breyer soon found itself fielding orders for more. The 'Western Horse' became Breyer's first standalone model horse.

The scale of that first model, 1:9 (a model at this scale stands around six to seven inches in height), became the standard for the company's 'Traditional' range, which soon began to feature famous horses from the world of racing, show jumping and even fiction. A range of other scales have also been introduced over the years, including the 1:12 Classic, 1:32 Stablemates and 1:64 Mini Whinnies.

As well as legendary horses such as Northern Dancer, Seabiscuit and Red Rum, the brand also celebrates the ordinary horses that bring joy to so many people, such as Strikey, who was chosen as the model to celebrate the 40th anniversary of the Riding for the Disabled Association. Fictional horses including Black Beauty and Michael Morpurgo's 'War Horse' have also found their way into the Breyer line-up.

Breyer molds are often used for multiple releases, with a horse potentially appearing in chestnut, gray, palomino and more colors. The fact that the horses are not articulated means they are just as likely to appeal as display items and collectibles as they are as playthings.

Black Beauty is one of Breyer's most enduring models, with many different versions emerging over the years. The horse changes subtly in each incarnation (there are different numbers of white 'socks' on each version, for instance).

Many molds serve to represent multiple horses. The 2004 Kentucky Derby and Preakness Stakes winner Smarty Jones has also seen service as Secretariat and Frankel, as well as many other generic horses, some of which were produced as one-off specials for charity auctions.

Around 20 people are involved in the creation of each Breyer horse. Leading sculptors in the field are employed to create the initial models, which are then converted into copper and steel molds. Cellulose acetate plastic is then poured into the molds to create the horses.

Playsets (such as the 1:32 scale Deluxe Animal Hospital set) add new elements to the range at the smaller scales, with vehicles, buildings, figures and other accessories available. The company also produces equestrian-themed jewelry and clothing for those who have been well and truly bitten by the Breyer bug.

THE LEGACY

Despite many other companies offering model horses of varying degrees of realism, Breyer is still going strong, with around 300 new products released each year. Each model is still hand-crafted, meaning that no two Breyer horses are identical.

Unsurprisingly, girls make up the largest share of the Breyer customer base, but boys are recognized as the quickest growing sector of the market. The annual Breyerfest event attracts around 4,000 people to Kentucky to celebrate the history of this classic range of models.

Having the Cozy Coupe be foot, rather than pedal-powered, was a smart move on two levels. Not only did it make the car available to younger children, it also helped keep manufacturing costs down.

Over the years, Little Tikes has attempted to capitalize on the success of the Cozy Coupe by expanding its range of vehicles to include pick-up trucks, convertibles and larger models. The original design remains timeless, though.

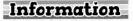

Cozy Coupe's enduring popularity and iconic design have earned it a place in Cleveland's Crawford Auto-Aviation Museum, where it sits proudly alongside the DeLorean, the Corvette, and the Model-T Ford.

THE LEGACY

Cozy Coupes are still on sale today, such as the Little Tikes 30th Anniversary Cozy Coupe. They have new features, such as a pretend ignition switch that turns and even a small boot to store toys in. But the basic design remains the same – Cozy Coupe is still a sturdy vehicle for children to run around in, causing mayhem indoors and outdoors.

Information

Manufacturer: Little Tikes
First Released: 1979
Expect to pay: $60

COZY COUPE

Everyone remembers their first car. The wheels spinning underneath you. The thrill of being in control of a hulking machine. The cool way of getting around, while those on foot gawk as you roll by. And that's just the experience you'll get from Cozy Coupe, which was the first car for many of us when we were younger.

The red and yellow vehicle was designed like a tiny Mini for one child to squeeze into, somewhat inevitable given it was created by a former car-parts designer for Chrysler. It had a fuel cap on the side, a single door that opened and a small seat inside. However, there was no engine to start or pedals to turn.

Without a motor of any kind, Cozy Coupe was powered by the driver's eager feet pushing along the ground through a small gap in the bottom of the car. Think of how the Flintstones used to drive, but cuter.

What made Cozy Coupe so popular was how well built it was, making it the safest choice for parents who wanted to get a play vehicle for their children. It was sturdy and felt like it could survive a meteor crash, let alone the minor bumps and scrapes a child gets while driving at Cozy Coupe's low speeds. It proved so popular that in 1991, Cozy Coupe was the biggest-selling car in the United States!

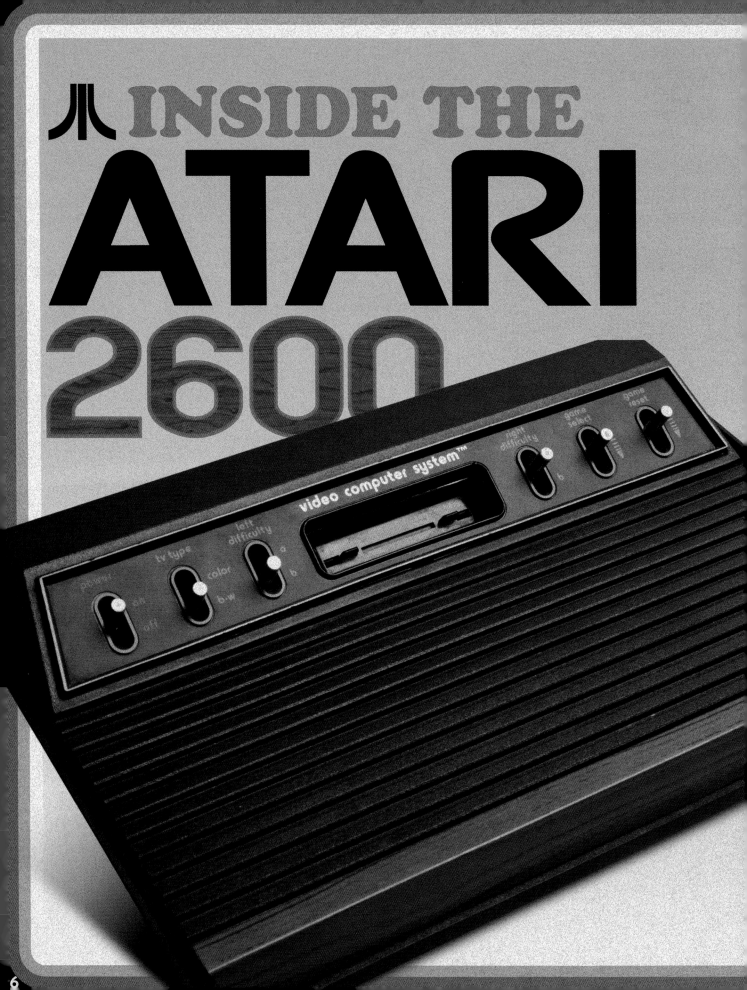

INSIDE THE
ATARI
2600

video computer system™

tv type · left difficulty · right difficulty · game select · game reset · power · on · off · color · b·w · a · b

The Atari 2600 is perhaps the most iconic console in early videogame history, and is so synonymous with the Atari brand that it's often simp ly referred to as 'the Atari'. Take a look behind the scenes at the creation and development of this industry-defining console

F or something that reached such lofty heights as the 2600 did, it should be understood that there were no great aspirations in mind when the synapses fired that led to it flickering into consciousness. It began as a humble idea; a simple, and inevitable next step – though one that would still take doing something never done before. "The architecture was pretty obvious to everybody," said project leader Al Alcorn, then head of consumer engineering. "The business was dedicated game chips, and obviously if you could get a microprocessor and a game in ROM, that was an idea that had legs to it."

What became the Atari 2600 began when Steve Mayer and Ron Milner were coming back from one of the many trips back and forth between their Cyan Engineering headquarters in Grass Valley and Atari Inc's base of operations in Los Gatos. Grass Valley was serving as Atari's R&D group for all its new coin-ops and related projects, a relationship that started in 1973. Cyan had been founded by Mayer and Larry Emmons – two engineers formerly of Ampex's Videofile division, the same stomping grounds as Atari co-founders Nolan Bushnell and Ted Dabney. As the coin-op videogame field began to quickly grow with competitors, Bushnell knew he needed to stay ahead of the competition by continually releasing new games. He soon struck up a working relationship with his former Ampex colleagues, and Cyan became an important part of his strategy. Enough so that he soon bought it outright. Cyan would build the wire-wrap prototypes for Atari's early Seventies arcade games, which were then sent down to Atari to be turned into the fully laid out production versions of the games. Quite often they were breaking new ground in their designs. As Nolan put it, "Cyan was building the technical stuff that people said couldn't be built."

It was during the summer of 1975 that Cyan would hit on its most important contribution, thanks to Mayer and Milner. The question they had been asking themselves on the trip back was whether or not they could leverage microprocessors to create a game console that could support multiple interchangeable games. The reason it was on their minds was because in several months Atari was poised to enter the consumer electronics market for the

first time. Pong was set to invade the home via a relationship with retailer Sears.

The move was made possible due to Atari engineer Harold Lee, who managed to cram Al Alcorn's entire original Pong arcade design into a single dedicated chip. Now, together with Sears' consumer electronics industry guidance and a new manufacturing plant paid for by investor Don Valentine, the Sears Tele-Games-branded home Pong would begin a new chapter in Atari's history. The company was already planning follow-up consoles based on the same innovative technology, looking to expand with home releases of the many Pong 'sequels' that it had put out in the arcade.

This is precisely what led to Milner and Mayer pondering the use of microprocessors for a future console. There was an obvious ceiling on the use of the 'Pong-on-a-chip' technology: you needed an entirely new custom chip each time you wanted a new set of games. Using a microprocessor meant you could simply use the same main chip and load new game software any time you wanted to play a different game.

As it turns out, management had also been pondering the idea but wanted to take it a step further. "Nolan, Joe [Keenan, Atari president] and I sat around as a team and decided we needed a cartridge-based game system," said Al. With Alcorn giving the go-ahead to Milner and Mayer to being the research, upon returning to the Cyan facilities the duo began investigating what microprocessors were available on the fledgling market to start basing their proof of concept around.

Knowledge Bank

LAUNCH DATE: 14 October 1977
LAUNCH PRICE: $199
DIMENSIONS: 13.625 x 9.125 x 3.5 in
WEIGHT: 4.625lbs
PROCESSOR: MOS/Signetics 6507 (running at 1.19MHz)
RAM: 128 bytes
DISPLAY: Between 256 and 320 pixels per line, and 192 to 240 lines per screen
COLORS: 128 NTSC, 104 PAL
ASSOCIATED MAGAZINES: Atari Age, Atari Club, Atari Owner's Club, Atarian

Choosing a microprocessor and a rebel named peddle

motorola and intel were the two leaders in the nascent microprocessor industry, which began four years earlier with the introduction of Intel's 4004 chip and was now maturing through Intel's 8080 and Motorola's 6800. With industry stalwarts Fairchild Semiconductor and Texas Instruments not far behind, sources for the technology seemed to be abundant.

Ron and Steve proceeded to put together several different wish lists for various experimental microprocessor-based game consoles, even going so far as to contact Motorola on pricing. The concept of the console itself went through a series of revisions at this time, including the possibility of producing several 'dedicated' versions, with a group of games built in to each through ROMs.

The problem for an engineer designing a new games console, though, was that the microprocessors currently on the market

HOW IT WORKS

A GUIDE TO THE KEY INTERNAL COMPONENTS THAT MAKE UP THE LAUNCH ATA

CARTRIDGE PORT
Besides being the location where game cartridges are plugged in, it also functions as an expansion port of sorts. Later items like keyboards and extra RAM used the cartridge port to interface with the 2600's internals.

CONTROLLER PORT
Two DB-9 ports used for plugging in a variety of controllers and peripherals. Their innovative use allowed the 2600 to have a multitude of potential controllers at a time when controls were normally hardwired to the console.

CONTROL SWITCHES
Housed on a separate PCB that's joined by a ribbon board, these are the iconic control switches used in of the 2600. These are (left to right) the power switch black and white), left difficulty, right difficulty, gam through the many game variations provided in a car 1980 the difficulty switches were dropped from the the back near the joystick ports. By the later launch the switches were replaced by plastic sliders.

TIA
Standing for television interface adaptor and originally known as Stella, this is the guts of the 2600's graphics and sound.

R/F M
The p
the TI
modu
chann
it mor
collec
the la
chann
chann
hole f
no act

CPU
The 2600's microprocessor is the 6507, an altered version of the venerable 6502. Missing some of the signal and interrupt lines from the 6502, it can address up to 8K memory natively – though later developers got around this with a technique called bank-switching. This microprocessor was also used as a floppy disk controller in Atari's later 8-bit computer line.

RIOT
An acronym for RAM-I/O-timer, it was more formally called the MOS Tech 6532. It includes the sole RAM on the 2600 – 128 bytes worth. The chip also reads the ports and the six control switches for the console.

SPEAKER RISER
Late in the design of the 2600, it was decided to switch from internally mounted speakers as in other mid-Seventies consoles to sending the audio out directly to the television set. The speaker risers present in the launch model show the decision came too late to change the molding of the case.

were still too expensive: around $100 to $300 each. A trip to the 1975 electronics industry convention, Wescon, that September would soon change that.

The Western Electronics Show and Convention (Wescon) was the premier electronics industry trade show in the US. Milner and Mayer just so happened to be doing their research shortly before the 24th annual Wescon, which was taking place in San Francisco that year. They decided to make the trip after receiving a letter from a new, unheard of company, inviting them to come take a look at its new microprocessor. They were soon to discover that the company was a young upstart in microprocessors, in an industry that was itself very young, and was poised to rock the foundation. What was that upstart? MOS Technology, which was led by Chuck Peddle.

Peddle was a former Motorola employee, joining the company in 1973 to finish its fledgling microprocessor project, based in Mesa, Arizona. After fixing flaws in Motorola's initial design for its first chip, the 6800, and designing the crucial support chip needed for its connection to peripheral devices, Peddle wanted to move on to do a second-generation, cost-reduced version. Unfortunately, Motorola wasn't interested in developing any more microprocessors at the time, so, undaunted, Peddle decided to pursue the development on his own. Eventually partnering with an old business acquaintance, John Pavinen, Peddle brought his project to John's company,

The upcoming Wescon was their target for the introduction and initial sales, and that August MOS Technology began placing ads in industry magazines, offering to sell a full microprocessor for $25 right there on the Wescon show floor. While the first half of the offer caught the public's eye, it was the latter that infuriated the Wescon organisers when they heard about it. Wescon was an industry trade show, not a flea market. Upon arriving to set up in their stand at the expo, Peddle and the MOS Technology people were promptly told that under no circumstances would they be selling their chips at the show where everyone in Silicon Valley would be coming to see it – including the guys from Cyan.

Being quick-thinking, Peddle came up with another solution. There was nothing prohibiting them from selling away from the show floor, nor mentioning where to go to buy the chips, so they used their booth for the standard presentation but directed people to their hotel suite to actually purchase the hardware. Peddle stationed his wife just outside the suite with a barrel of microprocessors and a stack of manuals. People would buy the chip and accompanying documentation from her, and then enter the suite to see the full series and support chips demonstrated by Peddle and company on fully functioning trainers (TIM and KIM-1), which they had also designed.

It wasn't long before a large line of hopeful engineers started developing, including a young man looking to build a personal

The launch version of the 2600 features a heavy duty thick plastic casing with characteristic curved edges, only seen on this model. In 1978 the look was changed to a much thinner and boxier style. Likewise the launch version includes six switches to control the power, color/black and white, left difficulty, right difficulty, game select and game reset settings. Also present in the 1978 model, in later versions of the 2600 the difficulty switches were moved to the back.

Initially the 2600 was to have all sound through internal speakers, but this was changed to go through the TV speakers after the case molds had been done. As such, the speaker holes in the 2600's top half and the speaker risers in the bottom half are still present. Some early revisions of the light 1978 model also have these present to various degrees.

The launch version of the 2600 is called the 'Heavy Sixer' by collectors. As seen here, it gets its name from the heavy metal shielding meant to block the electronic interference generated by the 2600. The FCC (Federal Communications Commission, the governing body in the US for regulating broadcasting) had not created its special class for devices like this yet, so the shielding was added to meet the current standards. The 1978 model left out the heavy shielding, and together with its cosmetic changes is sometimes referred to as the 'Light Sixer'. It's a common myth that only Heavy Sixers were made in Sunnyvale; the early runs of the Light Sixers were made there as well.

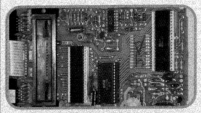

The motherboard of the 2600 is actually quite small, and besides the ribbon cable to the switch board and the cartridge port, it contains three main chips. (Left to right) The 6507 CPU, the MOS RIOT chip and the TIA graphics chip.

"Famicom microprocessors meant you could load new software to play a different game"

MOS Technology. MOS had been dying in the crowded calculator market, and the lure of a low-cost microprocessor proved too great to pass up. So, as Motorola was debuting its 6800 for $300 in August 1974, Peddle and seven co-workers were leaving to begin designs on its low-cost competitor.

Their goal was to sell the new chip in the $20 to $25 range, and offer a series of microprocessors and support chips. They decided to name the series '6500', to directly associate it with Motorola's 6800. The 6502 would be the main microprocessor in the series, which also included a series of support chips to allow connection to various peripherals, just as Peddle had pioneered at Motorola.

The joy of becoming a proud owner of this state-of-the-art gaming system during the holiday season of 1977. One of Joe Decuir's favorite moments was watching kids like this play his creation at a store display during the launch.

computer, Steve Wozniak. Also among the throngs of engineers were Milner and Mayer, who were both just as impressed with the barrel of microprocessors as the others in line were. Little did they know, though, that only the top half of the barrel contained working chips.

After getting their 6502 with documentation, the two headed in to see Peddle and his people demonstrating the trainers. They met and talked for about an hour and a half, finally negotiating with Peddle to come over to Cyan the next day to discuss plans for using MOS's 6502 and support chip in their proposed game system.

Peddle and his team headed over to Cyan, where they met and negotiated over the next two days. Steve and Ron's previous dream specs were discussed, as well as needs, possible board designs, and financial targets. In the end, Cyan decided to sign on with MOS Technology's chip, but not the 6502. Because it was targeted for a mass-produced game system, cost was an issue and the proposed 6507 was more in line to meet that goal. With the 6507 and the support chip, they'd just need to design a processor for dedicated graphics and sound support.

MOS had a relationship with another engineering firm by the name of Microcomputer Associates, which had developed the debugging software for MOS's training systems and had its own development system that was being publicly sold the following month, complete with a terminal interface and built-in debugging software.

10 GAMES THAT DEFINED THE ATARI 2600

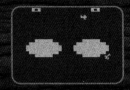

ADVENTURE
YEAR RELEASED: 1979

Warren Robnett's *Adventure* was a massively defining game and not just for the Atari 2600. In addition to being one of the earliest examples of a developer sneaking his name into a game, it also allowed players to stash items and went on to popularize the adventure genre, which has since been championed by everything from *Haunted House* to *The Legend Of Zelda*. It went on to sell 1 million units, which isn't bad for a game inspired by a text adventure.

E.T.
YEAR RELEASED: 1982

Howard Scott Warshaw's *E.T.* helped define the 2600 as well, but for all the wrong reasons. Originally envisioned by Warshaw as an innovative companion piece to the film, late negotiations for the rights meant that he had just five weeks to get the game ready for Christmas. Although it sold over 1.5 million units, Atari Inc actually ordered 4 million, and as a result had to send surplus copies back, with rumours that the cartridges were used as landfill born out in 2014.

YARS' REVENGE
YEAR RELEASED: 1982

In the same year that he created his most notorious game, Warshaw also shipped his best. Starting off as a port of Cinematronics' *Star Castle*, Warshaw remolded the game into something completely original. The end result was an amazingly innovative shooter that became so popular it even spawned its own theme song and a radio drama based around the comic book that featured the original story. It went on to become the bestselling original title for Atari's console.

SPACE INVADERS
YEAR RELEASED: 1980

There are few games as defining as Atari's port of *Space Invaders*. It was the first licensed arcade game, became the first console videogame to sell over a million units -- it eventually sold over 2 million in its first year -- and defined the term 'killer app' when its sheer popularity saw the 2600's sales quadruple after the game was released. Not bad for a machine that was already three years old at the time. Although not very arcade accurate, it sported 112 different gameplay variations.

COMBAT
YEAR RELEASED: 1977

Combat was inspired by *Tank*, but improved on the original arcade game by offering 27 different gameplay modes that were also inspired by other arcade games. Available as one of the Atari 2600's nine launch titles, it's remembered by virtually every 2600 owner, due to being the game that was actually packaged with the console. Steve Mayer, Joe Decuir, Larry Wagner and Larry Kaplan created one of the earliest examples of a two-player game on the machine.

"Motorola sued Peddle and MOS Technology for theft of engineering drawings and trade secrets"

Called the Jolt, it was decided to use this as the main board of the console during development of the custom chip.

One last hurdle remained. Both MOS and Atari/Cyan wanted to set up a second manufacturing source for the chips. MOS wanted it because setting up a second source would give it more credibility in the microprocessor market; Atari wanted it as a backup in case MOS went out of business, which would not be that uncommon. Atari also wanted to deal with someone on the West Coast, instead of out east where MOS was located. It turned out both companies had someone in mind, and both were thinking of the same company: Synertek.

Peddle had worked with the Synertek president and co-founder, Bob Schreiner, during their tenure at GE. He also knew Schreiner wanted to get into microprocessors and was more than happy to help his old friend out. Atari wanted to work with Synertek because they already had a working relationship – Synertek was the company doing the 'Pong-on-a-chip' IC layout and manufacturing.

With everything settled by the next month, Milner and Mayer notified the other microprocessor manufacturers that they were no longer interested in their products and were going with MOS instead. That was fine for most of the manufacturers, since the

Cyan contract was not considered the 'big money' deal they were looking for. Fine, that is, for all except one.

Motorola, which had kept an eye on Peddle, sued him and MOS Technology for theft of engineering drawings and trade secrets exactly one week after the announcement. Using the short turnaround time between Peddle's departure and the production run as evidence, and the fact that the 6501 model was pin-compatible with Motorola's 6800, it filed suit on 3 November 1975. Here was the exact reason why Atari wanted a second source, with the possibility of an injunction preventing MOS from doing any manufacturing. Motorola eventually won the suit, though not against the 6502. The terms called for the destruction of all 6501s and a payment of $300,000 for the legal fees. Though it would end up making the 6501 a very collectable chip for computer enthusiasts today, it was of little concern to Atari and Cyan at the time. They had their second source, an extremely cost-effective base design, and the talent to begin their next-generation gaming console.

A proofing stella

By December 1975, Milner and Mayer were able to get a working, although buggy, prototype to play a home version of Atari/

Kee's hit arcade game, *Tank*. Using the 6502/Jolt setup along with the beginnings of a custom graphics chip, the two had even appropriated the actual joysticks from a Tank coin-op for the primordial system's controls.

At that point, a young engineer was hired by Alcorn to help debug the project and bring it back from Cyan to Atari for its next stage, working as a bridge of sorts. Joe Decuir was a graduate of the local UC Berkeley and working in medical instrumentation design, and looking for a way out. "We were using expensive new equipment to try heroically to save people in really bad shape," he revealed. "Most of them – 91 percent – died either way. It was kind of demoralizing."

A friend of Decuir's, Ed DeWath, had known Milner and recommended Decuir for Cyan. Decuir actually wasn't sure about going into games, but luckily for all of us he was convinced by his father and another friend. "My father said, 'Pick the job that teaches you more,' and Cyan/Atari had the potential to teach chip design. My friend Greg said: 'You can do good for the world with games. Most people are sick by their own hand – smoking, bad eating, etc – and are lonesome and bored. Go ahead and entertain them.'"

Decuir immediately set about debugging the demo system, and one of the first things he had to do was have an account created on the DEC PDP-11 timesharing system the group was using for cross-assembling the demo game code. Needing a password, he chose the name of his favorite bike, Stella, which he still owns and rides to this day. The name would stick

SOME OF THE MOST IMPORTANT AND INFAMOUS TITLES TO BE RELEASED ON ATARI'S POPULAR HOME CONSOLE

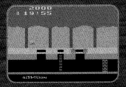

PITFALL!
YEAR RELEASED: 1982

Pitfall! was a massive deal on the 2600. It sold over 4 million units, becoming the second bestselling game on the system after *Pac-Man*. The game had its own cartoon show and helped establish Activision as a publishing force to be reckoned with. It's also one of the earliest examples of a scrolling platformer – games before it were static, single-screen affairs – and while Pitfall Harry wasn't an official Atari mascot, many gamers instantly associated him with the 2600 console.

RIVER RAID
YEAR RELEASED: 1982

Created by ex-Atari coder Carol Shaw, and based on Atari's 1978 coin-op *Sky Raider*, *River Raid* was another hit for the fledgling Activision and became the tenth bestselling game on the system, with sales of over 1 million. Like many Activision games it's an incredibly slick piece of coding that pushed the machine in ways that were rarely seen on the system. *River Raid* was an interesting shooter featuring rolling terrain that was dynamically generated during play.

MISSILE COMMAND
YEAR RELEASED: 1980

After the graphically disappointing *Space Invaders, Missile Command* proved that it was possible to create an extremely good reproduction of a hit arcade game on Atari's console. There were obviously compromises made to the game – it's missing the planes and UFOs, for example – but it's still an extremely fun game. It proved to be an equally big hit on the Atari 2600, eventually going on to sell over 2.5 million units, making it the system's fourth bestselling game.

THE EMPIRE STRIKES BACK
YEAR RELEASED: 1982

Although *The Empire Strikes Back* wasn't the first videogame to be based on a film or TV licence, it was the first to prove that it was possible to capture the excitement of the original product. The first ever game to be based on the *Star Wars* franchise saw you zooming around in a Snowspeeder while taking down Imperial AT-ATs. Extremely popular at the time and later converted to the Intellivision, it started a rich gaming franchise that continues to this day.

PAC-MAN
YEAR RELEASED: 1982

When *Pac-Man* was being created by Tod Frye, Atari was so sure of its success that it simply assumed 10 million 2600 owners would rush out and buy it. Not only that, but it thought more people would buy the machine to play it (it was a pack-in title), leading Atari to order 12 million units on the assumption that predicted sales would reach $500 million. The plan backfired, and while it shifted 7 million units, it created a massive number of unsold carts, which many attribute Atari Inc's eventual fate to.

---

and eventually become the code name for the 2600's custom graphics chip, but in the meantime Decuir's goal was getting the *Tank* game further along in time for a February 1976 demonstration to Bushnell, Keenan and Alcorn. The prototype's architecture at that time was influenced by the coin-op arcade game design that Cyan had also done for Atari. That would certainly make sense, given that the goal of the 2600 was to play all Atari's early and mid-Seventies coin-op games.

In essence, it was a minimalist version of the features present in Atari's coin-ops. Everything was synced to the scan lines of the television display. What was to be displayed on the screen was then supported by separate hardware registers for the screen elements that were themselves split up. A separately generated background filed with 'stamped' graphic items was termed as the 'playfield' – a term borrowed from pinball. The objects that were player-controlled or interactive were termed player/missile objects and used separate hardware object generation known today as 'sprites'. In this case, each object to be displayed would be generated separately by loading the

individual pixel descriptions for each into several hardware registers. Both the playfield and player registers could be reused by the programmer per each scan line, meaning you could have multiple player objects – a concept done to keep costs down but that would ultimately lead to a very flexible system that allowed graphics capabilities far beyond what was originally envisioned.

When February rolled around, also on the agenda for that day was a demonstration of a prototype videophone system that Cyan had designed. However, only one of the two would make it past approval stage for full product design down at Atari, as Bushnell hilariously dismissed the videophone by mooning the team through it.

Now that the project was approved to move on and come down from Cyan to Atari, Atari knew it was going to have to bring someone on board to design the full custom graphics chip. None of the engineers in the coin division would be up to the task of the advanced custom chip layout design called VLSI (very-large-scale integration). Likewise, Harold Lee, who had designed the custom 'Pong-on-a-chip' that launched Atari's consumer division, didn't feel he

The man behind the 6502, Chuck Peddle also helped spec out the proof of concept for the 2600 and find a second source to manufacture his chips for Atari.

was up to the task either. "You could pack a lot more logic in when dynamic logic became available," he explained. "I'd never designed a chip like that before, so I didn't want to do that, and that's when I brought Jay Miner to do it since he'd already had experience in designing those chips."

Alcorn and Lee had known about Miner because of his previous work on helping them with the 'Pong-on-a-chip' layout at Synertek. Now, after setting up Synertek as a major secondary

REVISIONS, REVISIONS...

THE 2600 WENT THROUGH SEVERAL REVISIONS DURING ITS TIME ON THE MARKET, AS WELL AS HAVING ALTERNATIVE VERSIONS AVAILABLE THROUGH SEARS UNDER ITS TELE-GAMES LABEL

HEAVY SIXER
The original 1977 model with its six console levers, thick molded plastic, heavy internal shielding, faux woodgrain and deluxe controllers. Notable for being manufactured in Sunnyvale.

LIGHT SIXER
Released between 1978 and 1980. Cost-reduced exterior and joysticks.

2600-A
Four-switch model, difficulty switches moved to the back. Last model with woodgrain effect.

2600
Four-switch all-black model called the 'Darth Vader' by collectors. First actual use of 2600 as the name of the console instead of its model number, mainly because of the simultaneous release of the Atari 5200 in 1982.

ATARI 2800
Released 1983. Rare Japanese version of the 2600. Released in the US as the Sears Video Arcade II.

2600 JR
Released in 1985. The final revision, extremely cost reduced.

Clockwise starting top right: Atari 2800, 2600-A with Spectravideo CompuMate computer expansion, Heavy Sixer, unreleased Kee Games prototype version.

---

source for the 6502 chip, which was fast gaining popularity, Alcorn used that as leverage for prying Miner away. Promising large chip orders in the near future, as Atari was beginning to use the 6502 in coin-ops as well, he was able to get Miner under an Atari badge. Decuir had already been notified after the February demonstration that he was moving down to Atari, and with Miner on board, he'd be apprenticing directly under the man Alcorn described as being "the best chip layout guy on the planet". Together they would be leading the transition from the Cyan proof-of-concept to a fully produced game console, complete with the first-of-its-kind custom graphics chip. Larry Wagner was also added as head of software development, and he would eventually be in charge of hiring the programmers who did the first ten launch games – many of whom would later go on to form Activision, the world's first independent games developer.

adaptor), several major occurrences happened that would affect it both in the immediate and long term.

First and foremost was the sale of Atari Inc to Warner Communications, completed in October 1976. Atari had been in dire straits financially and had been looking for people to invest and inject much-needed cash to allow the company to continue to grow. When that didn't work, Bushnell and Keenan began looking for someone to sell the company to outright, and Warner came knocking with its deep pockets.

Second to happen was Atari's settlement with Magnavox in the beginning of June 1976 over patent lawsuits. Agreeing to pay a large sum and give free access to any Atari technology already produced or in production until June 1977, hiding the 2600 – now called the Video Computer System – was crucial. As such, the revolutionary games console didn't make an appearance at the Consumer

"Everything in the VCS pointed to a high-end piece of entertainment equipment"

Most of the engineering for the consumer division, since it was still just a small group of people, was taking place among their coin-op division colleagues. After all, Atari had just started its foray into the consumer arena, and its main bread and butter at that time was still arcade games. Alcorn knew that Atari needed to keep the revolutionary console a secret from competitors, but also, more importantly, from a lot of management: "My job was to keep the hounds away from these guys, to keep away the corporate bean counters and just let them do their job, which was about 50 percent of my time."

He rented a secret location far away on Division Street to let the expanded team do their work. That didn't last long, as without telling him, head of coin-op engineering Steve Bristow rented the building right next door for Atari's new pinball operations.

Stella to Video Computer System

Under Miner's leadership, the 2600's architecture was formalized, restructuring the internal memory map and planned hardware registers, and making sure the synchronization between the 6507 and the custom graphics chip was so tight that there was less memory needed. RAM was costly for the time, so the console would have to make do with the 128 bytes on the 2600's third chip, which was called RIOT (RAM-I/O-Timer).

The custom graphics chip had now been renamed Stella by Miner after seeing Decuir's use of it, and soon Miner's boss, Bob Brown, used it for the name of the entire project. In the meantime, Miner and Decuir took the bare-bones graphics processing done on the original prototype and began producing a gate-level version, which would be the exact one that carried over into chip form. By the time it was finished and moved into its early chip format, where it was renamed TIA (television interface

Electronics Show until after the deadline had passed.

Last was the release of Fairchild's microprocessor-based system in August of 1976. With Fairchild in the area and several engineers at Atari being friends with the system's designer, Jerry Lawson, they knew the console was coming. Jerry was even able to solve the issue on his console that had been plaguing Atari's design team, which was guarding against static discharge when removing cartridges – an answer that Atari quickly employed. But now, with Fairchild hitting the market first, it was clear where the future of home consoles lay. And as far as Manny Gerard, the new overseer of Atari for Warner, was concerned, the future of Atari was the 2600. Warner had that much faith in it.

By the time it was finally shown off in June 1977, the 2600 had taken on the characteristics of the flagship product Warner demanded and Atari wanted. A mix of heavy, stylized plastic and faux woodgrain designed by Doug Hardy and Fred Thompson, it was meant to fit visually into anyone's entertainment center. It also featured a pair of deluxe arcade-style controllers to fulfil the requirements of playing the bulk of Atari's early arcade games – digital joysticks and analogue paddles – designed by Gerald Aamoth and John Hayashi. Also of note to those who saw it at the show was that, unlike Fairchild's console or any of the many *Pong* machines on the market, the 2600's sound was coming directly through the television's speakers instead of an internal speaker. With the much clearer sound output and the overall production value, everything pointed to a high-end piece of entertainment equipment.

Debuting in stores on 14 October 1977 with a set price of $199, Atari had immediately sold out of its entire initial 400,000-unit production run to retailers for that Christmas season. The consumer age at Atari had begun, and for millions of homes it was soon to be the Atari age.

DISSECTING THE ATARI 2600 JOYSTICK

IT'S ONE OF THE MOST ICONIC CONTROLLERS AROUND AND IS ARGUABLY AS ASSOCIATED WITH ATARI AS THE 2600 ITSELF. JOIN US, THEN, AS WE LOOK AT ONE OF THE MOST RECOGNIZABLE JOYSTICKS OF ALL TIME

The deluxe nature of the CX-10 is readily apparent with the use of heavy springs for all four directional contacts and the fire button to provide an arcade-like floating feel to the stick.

Most fans are not aware that the launch version of the 2600 included a special joystick only seen with this model. Designated the CX-10, as with the console case, this model is a deluxe version. Seen here on the left compared to the more common CX-40 joystick on the right, the immediate difference is the presence of a heavy-duty rubber grip, complete with inlaid Atari logo. Also note the absence of the 'top' designation added to the CX-40s to help out confused first-time users.

The 2600 joysticks, synonymous with Atari when you think of game controllers, were inspired by Atari/Kee Games' hit 1974 arcade game, *Tank*. With the original proof of concept of the 2600 based around playing a home version of the game, and with *Tank* included with the unit on the pack-in cartridge, *Combat*, the need to do so was obvious.

On the inside, the shapes of the controller PCB also differ in looks and layout, with the CX-10's six connectors split three by three.

The CX-40 instead uses a hard plastic disc to make contact with the controller PCB, giving it its more characteristic stiff feeling. The fire button still includes a spring, but it's a much lighter spring, providing less feedback than those on the CX-10.

ATARI AS ITS OWN COMPETITOR

NOT KNOWN BY MANY, ATARI ACTUALLY WORKED ON TWO ALTERNATIVE SYSTEMS TO THE 2600

Al Alcorn in the early Seventies. By the time of the 2600's design, Al was head of consumer engineering and overseeing Atari's expansion into its successful home products.

The first was a system that never saw regular production, called the Atari Game Brain. Meant as an alternative to the 2600's microprocessor-based architecture, each cartridge contains all the circuitry for each game. The console itself is almost empty, containing only wiring for the controls and hookups.

At first glance, the Game Brain looks like an attempt to cram every single control scheme in Atari's arcade games onto the surface of the console, with four direction buttons in lieu of joysticks. In fact, a Rolodex-style stack of cards was provided to show which buttons were used for each of the five initial games: *Video Music, Ultra Pong, Super Pong, Stunt Cycle* and *Video Pinball*.

Although it was canceled, consoles with the same concept of full dedicated console hardware inside removable cartridges found their way onto the market in the form of the Coleco Telstar Arcade in the US and the SD-050 by Hanimex in Europe.

Atari also hedged its bets on the future of the market with a dedicated home version of its *Tank* coin-op called *Tank II*. The console featured hardwired versions of the same joysticks planned for the 2600 and was actually shown alongside the 2600 at the June 1977 CES. When it was clear that the 2600 was in demand for the upcoming Christmas season, *Tank II* was unceremoniously dumped.

▶

Backstories were provided for the original robot pugilists. The 'rollicking' Red Rocker hailed from Soltarus II, while the 'beautiful' Blue Bomber was the Pride of Umgluck. They weighed 375 and 382 pounds respectively (that's well over 26 stone each).

Information

Manufacturer: Marx
First Released: 1965
Expect to pay: $60-150

ROCK 'EM SOCK 'EM ROBOTS

The combative nature of the game has made it a staple for satire, with the heads of well-known politicians, sportspersons or other celebrities (like one featuring actress Bette Midler and TV host Geraldo Rivera from America's Tonight Show in 1992) substituted for hilarious comic effect.

The game was originally meant to feature human combatants, but it proved difficult to make them look realistic and development was shelved after the death of boxer Davey Moore in 1963. The idea to switch to robot boxers (the brainwave of inventor Burt Meyer) allowed the concept to move forward.

The best playthings often seem to come at a price. With skateboards it's skinned elbows, while with Etch A Sketch, it's calloused fingers. The price for playing Rock 'Em Sock 'Em Robots, however, was a pair of sore thumbs as you strove to deliver the haymaker that would knock your opponent's block off and win the 'Championship of the Universe' for your robot.

The Red Rocker and Blue Bomber were tireless fighting machines, and they would happily step back into the ring just moments after getting knocked out. The poor old human 'managers' controlling them were often not as durable and when thumbs got too tired to deliver the punches, players would often resort to simply slamming the controls with the palm of their hand. Still, this was boxing, so it wasn't meant to be pain-free.

The game was inspired by a trip to a Chicago amusement arcade by inventors Marvin Glass and Burt Meyer. A boxing-themed game piqued their interest, and they set about planning a smaller version for use in the home. One of the biggest stumbling blocks – getting the fighters to fall over when punched – was neatly (and dramatically) sidestepped by having the robots' heads jump up instead.

The original release of the toy included scorecards so that round-by-round progress could be charted – each round would continue until a knockout blow was landed. Some movement was possible, but the real fun lay in standing toe-to-toe and trading blows.

'Rock 'Em Sock 'Em Robots' is an impressive enough name, but when marketed in the UK the producers went one better, rechristening it 'Raving Bonkers' and adopting the legendary advertising slogan, "We're all mad about Raving Bonkers." It was no idle boast, either; the toy was a best-seller for over a decade.

"When thumbs got too tired to deliver punches, players would often resort to slamming the controls with the palm of the hand"

THE LEGACY

Mattel's relaunched version, which came out in 2000, was considerably smaller than the original (think of them as lightweights rather than heavyweights), which was an issue considering a big slice of the market comprised grown-ups reveling in a little toy nostalgia – the smaller controls weren't great for larger adult hands. Various themed versions have also been launched including Buzz Lightyear versus Emperor Zurg and the obvious Megatron versus Optimus Prime. The toy has also made the leap into the world of videogames.

© Shutterstock

THE LEGACY

Dubreq was reformed in 2003 by Brian Jarvis' son, Ben, and it continues to make Stylophones today. It resurrected the instrument in 2007 and has sold almost a million in the time since. Today, it continues to enjoy a cult following, playing not only on nostalgia but the eccentricity of the sound. A prominent user is Victoria Hesketh, aka the electropop singer-songwriter and DJ Little Boots. She can be watched playing the instrument on stage during her tours.

▼

Created as a toy synthesizer, the stylophone was made by Dubreq Studios, which was the name of the company owned by Brian Jarvis with his brother Ted and friend Burt Coleman. Dubreq is a combination of 'dubbing' and 'recording' but with a 'q' in place of the 'c'.

▶

Dubreq wanted the synthesizer to be cheap to manufacture so that as many people as possible would buy and use it. Not having physical keys helped to lower the costs, as did opting for a simple black and silver finish, even though fake wood veneers appeared on later models for those wanting added 'style'.

▶

In the 1970s (before being convicted of sexual offences), musician Rolf Harris was a much-loved entertainer at the top of his game. He put his face to the Stylophone and showed people how to use it in an artistic, experimental manner – a move that saw Dubreq's sales soar to an ear-piercing 3 million.

Information

Manufacturer: Dubreq
First Released: 1968
Expect to pay: $3

▲

So many musicians made use of the Stylophone, from David Bowie on his debut *Space Oddity* to Kraftwerk, Tony Visconti, Queen and The Osmonds. Pulp helped to make it popular again in 1992 when they used on their song *Styloroc (Nites of Suburbia)*, which formed a B-side to their single Babies.

STYLOPHONE

lthough heavy metal gained a cult following during the 1970s, the decade also rocked to a rather different sound. That's because Brian Jarvis had invented a stylus-operated pocket synthesizer better known as a Stylophone and the idiosyncratic instrument struck a chord with 3 million fans.

It certainly helped that some of the big stars of the day were fond of the organ and its single-setting speaker. Popsters such as David Bowie would strike the metal keys with gusto, closing a circuit with a voltage-controlled oscillator to release the well-known tinny notes associated with the device. *Space Oddity* may not have been the same without it.

Indeed, for so many kids, it was their first taste of making music, but Jarvis' invention was accidental. He had been fixing his niece's electric piano only to note that some of the dislodged keys could be placed on to a single circuit. Using a metal pen, he discovered that different notes could be made and this, he mused, would make an easy-to-learn instrument, even though the sound that it emitted was far from sophisticated.

As such, three variants ended up being produced. Of these (standard, bass and treble), the standard version was most popular. Like the others, it had a vibrato control on the front but it didn't have the 'wah-wah' effect of the larger 350S, which also came with more notes and an extra stylus. Despite the range's success, however, the plug was pulled in 1975. Most likely because parents wished we'd turn that racket off and play something more soothing instead.

© Alex Ashbourne, Getty Images

DUNGEONS & DRAGONS

Discover how Gary Gygax and Dave Arneson created a game that's as relevant today as it was four decades ago

How it began

Before there were dungeons, or even dragons for that matter, there was Jeff Perren. Perren was a game designer, a friend of the late Gary Gygax and a member of the Lake Geneva Tactical Studies Association (as Gygax was). When the convention received a large number of Elastolin figures, it inspired Perren to create a new set of rules which focused on mass combat. Gygax took the base rules, added a fantasy twist and made some tweaks, with the end result being published as Chainmail. The late Dave Arneson was well aware of Chainmail, because he was using it while playing Braunstein, an unpublished Napoleonic game that was set in the fictional town of Braunstein. It was more focused on individual play as

opposed to the popular mass combat games of the time and Arneson was using Chainmail's combat system. He started adding additional mechanics like levels, experience points, armor class and other important elements which would define the genre for years to come, and eventually made his way to Gygax.

Gygax began crafting a world and rule set to house all the interesting mechanics that Arneson had created and he took inspiration from a huge variety of sources. History, world mythology and pulp fiction all played important parts for Gygax while he was creating his new universe, but fantasy novels, particularly *The Lord Of The Rings*, would prove to be one of the most valuable resources. Copyright action from Tolkien Enterprises meant Gygax had to change a number of creatures and races, so Hobbits became Halflings, Ents became Treants and so on, leading Gygax to downplay the importance of Tolkien's influence on his game (although he eventually admitted that the

books had "a strong impact" on him in a 2000 interview).

Literature continued to shape Dungeons & Dragons with various monsters, spells and magical items coming from the works of Lewis Carroll, Edgar Rice Burroughs, HP Lovecraft, Fletcher Pratt, Michael Moorcock and many, many others. Jack Vance's *Dying Earth* series heavily influenced how wizards would memorize their spells, while Poul Anderson's *Three Hearts And Three Lions* would form the basis of D&D's alignment system. Even the Book Of Genesis provided inspiration, with the flaming sword described in it inspiring the clerical spell, Blade Barrier.

The first version of Dungeons & Dragons was released across a set of three booklets in 1974. Despite being rather basic looking and needing a heavy reliance on familiarity with wargaming it became a considerable success, easily selling over 1,000 copies in its first year of release. Gygax and Arneson had created something truly special, but it was only going to get bigger…

MOST DESIRABLE!

Dungeons & Dragons Basic Set

First released in 1977, TSR's gateway entry into the world of D&D really came alive with its third revision in 1983. Housed in a gorgeous red box, it included a 64-page Players Manual, a 48-page Dungeon Masters Rulebook, six dice and stunning artwork by Larry Elmore.

Widely available in all sorts of locations (even high profile high street shops sold it) it was instantly recognizable and was designed to take characters up to level three. Four additional sets were available, which would eventually take heroes all the way to immortality status. Fortunately, it's relatively cheap to pick up nowadays, with the 1983 version selling for around $25.

ESSENTIAL MERCH!

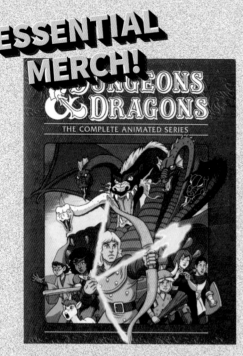

The Complete Animated Series

The adventures of Hank the ranger, Bobby the barbarian and Presto the wizard were essential viewing to any kid that grew up in the early 1980s and it's now possible to get every single episode on a complete DVD boxset. It even reveals the outcome of the final, unproduced finale, Requiem.

Ravenloft

There are countless brilliant AD&D modules, but one of the best is easily this 1983 offering by Tracy and Laura Hickman. Effectively their own take on Count Dracula, it became so popular that TSR turned it into a campaign setting in 1990. It now sells for around the $30 mark.

Planescape: Torment

This exceptional adventure game from 1999 is not only considered to be the best D&D videogame adaptation of all time, but one of the best Western RPGs. Coded by Black Isle Studio, it features a deep, gripping story and incredibly memorable characters. An enhanced version was recently released by Beamdog in 2017.

Going global

In 1977, TSR, the owners of Dungeons & Dragons, introduced a brand new concept for playing D&D. While it divided the user base in some ways and caused various issues along the way, it arguably helped popularize the company's game and helped bring it to even more people. TSR essentially split Dungeons & Dragons in half. There was a basic set, which was put together by J Eric Holmes, as well as Advanced Dungeons & Dragons, a more complex version of the game which was targeted at advanced hobby gamers and overseen by Gygax. It meant that TSR not only had the perfect springboard for those eager to try its new game, but was also able to appeal to long-term gamers who were looking for a fresh challenge. Many of the rules contradicted each other, but the lighter tone and structure of the basic set made it perfect and it was soon being found throughout the United States and numerous other countries. The rules for Advanced Dungeons & Dragons were spread across three core books (a concept that remains to this day): The Player's Handbook, The Dungeon Master's Guide and the Monster Manual. As more and more people became interested in the game, TSR released all sorts of expansion adventures (called modules) and campaign settings, for those gamers who were too lazy, or simply didn't have the time, to create their own wondrous worlds.

D&D really came of age during the 1980s with films like *ET The Extra-Terrestrial* and a D&D TV show, which ran from 1983 to 1985. All sorts of campaign worlds were introduced during the period, including Mystara, Dragonlance, Grayhawk and Forgotten Realms (which remains the most popular setting to this day) and countless new rule books were released. Novels based around the campaign worlds grew in popularity and numerous videogames started to appear also. Its success drew controversy however, particularly from Christian groups who claimed it promoted witchcraft, pornography, murder, suicide and Satanism. More bad publicity came after the press linked the disappearance of 16-year-old James Dallas Egbert III to the game and the one-woman crusade of Patricia Pulling, who founded Bothered About Dungeons & Dragons after her son committed suicide. He was an active player of the game and the lawsuit she filed against TSR led both her and Gary Gygax to appear on *60 Minutes*.

When TSR revised its rule set in 1989, it took the opportunity to remove all references to demons, devils and other potentially offensive supernatural entities. Demons became known as tanar'ri, while devils were known as baatezu. The controversy had played its hand however, and D&D began to be confined to specialist hobby shops.

In the subsequent decades the game continued to evolve and change. Most notably its publisher, and original owner, TSR, was acquired by Wizards Of The Coast, the owners of the popular collectible card game, Magic: The Gathering. New campaigns were introduced, novels based on the various game worlds continued to be popular and videogames continued to evolve. D&D continued to be referred to in popular culture and has had something of a renaissance in the last decade thanks to brilliant references in shows like *Community* and *Stranger Things*, as well as popular podcasts like Critical Role.

Now in its fifth edition, Dungeons & Dragons shows no signs of slowing down and its rich rule set, emphasis on working together with a group of like-minded people, and sheer creativity continues to excite gamers to this day. It's astonishing to think that after nearly 45 years the creation of Gary Gygax and Dave Arneson is stronger than ever.

Collector's guide

The sheer breadth and diversity of Dungeons & Dragons means there's pretty much something for everyone. Want to play an apocalyptic version of D&D? Then you'll want to track down Dark Sun. Fancy playing in an *Arabian Nights* campaign setting? Then Al-Qadim is the perfect set for you. Horror fans can delve into the excellent Ravenloft, sci-fi fans can try out the short-lived Spelljammer campaign, while those interested in more traditional settings can seek out the likes of Grayhawk, Dragonlance and Forgotten Realms; there really is something for everybody.

There are a wide range of videogames based in D&D universes, some of which are slowly rising in price and include the likes of the *Eye Of The Beholder* games and the *Baldur's Gate* series. As with anything collectible, it's typically super-popular items or the ones that failed first time around that go for the most money, but fortunately, even first edition books of D&D can be picked up relatively cheaply, and it's often the modular adventures that tend to go for more money. Because the rules of D&D have constantly evolved over the years, certain players will favor certain rule sets, which can again keep costs down. Basically, if you are interested in entering the exciting world of D&D, there's never been a better time to discover it.

"Bad publicity came with the one-woman crusade of Patricia Pulling, who founded Bothered About Dungeons & Dragons after her son committed suicide"

PADDINGTON BEAR

Paddington Bear's origins go back to 1956, but the first stuffed toy based on the character did not appear for another 16 years. By then, Michael Bond had already written many of his much-loved books, the first of which was *A Bear Named Paddington*.

Accompanied by beautiful drawings from the pen of illustrator Peggy Fortnum, it had been inspired by a toy bear Bond had purchased at Selfridges for his wife. He'd named it after the London railway station and loved it to bits – just as those who got their hands on Paddington did in 1972.

First to show interest in creating Paddington Bears was a small company called Gabrielle Designs, which had been started by Shirley and Eddie Clarkson from a spare room of their home. It was rather fitting that they should take this task upon themselves, given the quintessentially British nature of the character, and the bears were an instant success, bringing great joy to thousands of children.

It was they who cemented the look of the trademark hat, duffle coat and Wellington boots, the latter in particular proving so crucial because they allowed the bear to stand. There may have been no battered suitcase accompanying the toy, and children would have to imagine Paddington's penchant for marmalade, but the bears flew off the shelves. Indeed, according to Shirley, who wrote a book about the toy called *Bearly Believable: My Part In The Paddington Bear Story*, retailers from across the world wanted to sell the bear and the company struggled to keep up with demand.

Even so, there were some problems with 50,000 bears having faulty eyes, while a strike by the workforce caused supplies to stutter. But kids were oblivious to all of that and Paddington wouldn't be Paddington without a few scrapes. Indeed, children enjoyed being close to the beloved bear and they looked after him well: just as the luggage tag around his neck asked them to.

▲

The best-selling year for Paddington Bear stuffed toys was 1978, with Gabrielle Designs seeing as many as 87,000 being snapped up. Sadly, the company closed just 20 years later, even though it was still making Paddington Bear toys. Critics suggested the bear had been usurped by rival characters such as the Teletubbies.

▼

Although Yorkshire-based Gabrielle Designs made Paddington Bears in the United Kingdom, another company called Eden Toys manufactured them in the United States. These were created from 1975 and they were also based on Michael Bond's fabulous series of books.

▶

Original Paddington Bears by Gabrielle Designs were made with acrylic fur and had boots made by wellie-makers Dunlop. They also had orange eyes and a plastic dog-like nose. They would come with an assortment of outfits, making them rather collectible, though the duffle coat was always a favorite.

Information

Manufacturer: Gabrielle Designs
First Released: 1972
Expect to pay: $150

▲

The first person to receive a Paddington Bear stuffed toy was a 12-year-old boy called Jeremy Clarkson, who received his gift in 1971. Many will know him as the former presenter of Top Gear, but back then he was simply the son of Shirley and Eddie – the couple who ran Gabrielle Designs, the company that eventually got the licence for toys based on the character.

Please look after this bear. Thankyou

THE LEGACY

As well as Michael Bond's books, Paddington Bear hit the small screen courtesy of the BBC, which premiered its debut series in 1976. It made 56 episodes in total and followed them up with specials in the 1980s. Further series were then made with the most recent being in 1997. But in 2014, a hugely successful movie was released, sparking a sequel in 2017. StudioCanal is now working on a new TV series based on those live-action films.

113

The US version, Big Trak, had a few design differences, including a smart silvery gray color scheme, which somehow gave it a more militaristic appearance. There were also several differences on the control panel, including a 'HOLD' button, as compared with the 'P' (for pause) on the UK model.

An optional trailer was available, which Big Trak would happily drag along behind it, dumping the contents by means of the 'OUT' button on the control pad. The US Big Trak also had an 'IN' button on its control pad, which had no apparent use but spawned several conspiracy theories.

BIG TRAK

A sci-fi boom at the tail-end of the 1970s saw shops flooded with hi-tech (for the time) gadgets and toys, and a six-wheeled electronic behemoth stood proudly at the top of the heap.

Marketed as 'Big Trak' in the UK and 'Big Trak' in the States, this was a combination planetary explorer/space-age tank, rumbling along on chunky wheels and wielding a photon cannon for dealing with uncooperative aliens (or possibly merely blasting rock samples). Only the middle wheel on each side was powered, but this was enough to give Big Trak a decent range of maneuverability.

The ace up Big Trak's sleeve, however, was the new-fangled notion of programmability. Some of the numbers associated with the toy's processing 'power'

are difficult to comprehend. Its 64 bytes of 4-bit RAM seem ludicrously lightweight today, and when coupled with a bus speed of just 0.2 MHz you can begin to understand why the chip used in Big Trak was also commonly found in humble calculators.

Nevertheless, this was enough to allow the space-age traveller to accept 16 separate commands and execute them in the correct order. Commands were as unglamorous as turn left, move forwards and turn right, but it's surprising how entertaining it was to attempt to program Big Trak to move down a hallway, enter a room and blast whoever happened to be in there.

The computing power may have been primitive, but the designers were definitely onto something – Big Trak still looks pretty good 40 years later.

THE LEGACY

Big Trak won plenty of admirers, inspiring cloned versions in the Soviet Union, and it retained a certain cult collectability for decades after its initial release.

In 2010 Zeon Ltd brought out a replica Big Trak, lovingly modeled on the original, and more relaunches have followed. Dubreq (famous for its Stylophone) produced a half-size Big Trak Jr, while a Big Trak XTR, capable of being controlled using a smartphone or PC, has been in the pipeline for several years now.

Information

Manufacturer: Milton Bradley
First Released: 1979
Expect to pay: $20

▼

One of the obvious weaknesses of Big Trak was its inability to sense obstacles and navigate itself around them. It simply tried to go exactly where it was programmed to go. The Russian clone, the 'Lunokhod', actually included a sensor in its front bumper, but this simply terminated the program if an obstacle was encountered.

bigtrak

MB ELECTRONICS

▲

The original Big Trak had a tiny light bulb functioning as its mighty photon cannon (modern reboots make use of more durable LED lights) and it also beeped every 30 seconds when inactive to remind you to switch it off and conserve battery life.

© Big Trak, Sergio Calleja, Martin Ling

115

HUNGRY HIPPOS

Information

Manufacturer: Milton Bradley
First Released: 1978
Expect to pay: $10-15 (reprint), $30-35 (original)

Board games have grown and evolved a lot in the last few decades but even so, there remains something oddly cathartic in the stress-relieving chaos of Hungry Hippos. The game itself couldn't be simpler – just pick a colored hippo, jam on its tail lever to extend and retract the head, and devour as many marbles as possible while other players try to do the same.

The game is actually supposed to be played by releasing just a single marble at a time and fighting to see who can gobble it up before releasing another, but *nobody* ever played it like that. Instead, it's always a free-for-all with all 20 marbles in the dish from the beginning – or at least rapidly fired into play as the game begins – and panicked tail-mashing ensues.

Parents at the time soon came to a terrifying realization that the adverts never made apparent – Hungry Hippos is *loud*. The rattle of the balls pinging around the board, the mechanical clattering of both tail-smacking and heads repeatedly hitting the plastic base, the shouts and screams of players as the madness intensifies… it's a purchase decision that many parents no doubt regretted, even if it did bring us many hours of childhood joy.

Of course, it wasn't all good news. Balls sent flying by overeager hippos would often get lost, mechanisms had a habit of sticking and the very nature of the game meant that there were only so many poundings it could endure at the hands of excitable children, leading to many copies getting broken. Cue sighs of relief from parents the world over.

Even though it makes no difference which hippo you pick, MB decided to give them all names anyway – Homer (green), Harry (yellow), Henry (orange) and Lizzie/Happy (purple/pink), depending on the version.

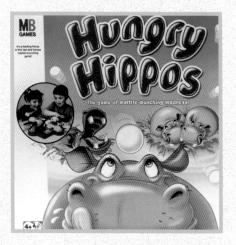

The hippos' heads are on a simple plastic pin hinge (some sets actually came disassembled), meaning overly aggressive play could lead to heads snapping off.

The game can be over in less time than it takes to get it out and set it up, and it's really not compelling enough (for anyone over five, at least) to play for more than a few minutes.

Given the tendency for balls to go missing, resourceful parents found that these could be replaced with regular glass marbles of the correct size. Which made the game even louder.

THE LEGACY

This classic game has been re-released and copied countless times over the years – we've seen everything from frogs and dinosaurs to dragons and farm animals replace the titular hippos, the last of those being an official FarmVille game. There's been something of a craze for recreating the game in real life, too. Players team up in pairs, one lying on a mat or skateboard with a bucket or similar receptacle for grabbing the large balls, with the second pushing and pulling the lying player by the feet so they can reach and return their balls. Craziness…

© Whitebox Mc

Fashion Fever

The looks, styles and fashion icons of an unforgettable decade

When it comes to the history of fashion, few decades possessed the sheer style confidence of the 1970s. It's an era that brings to mind some of the most iconic clothing items ever worn, each one intrinsically tied to the age of disco. Bell-bottoms. Platform shoes. Flares. Suits with giant lapels. It's so vibrant and clear in the mind, it almost feels like a uniform. But the fashion of the 1970s was anything but conformist.

These were ten years of styles and fashion statements that expressed individuality above anything else. Hairstyles and wardrobe items from past decades were back in, mixed with other pieces to create a seemingly endless myriad of trends. The music and the cinema of that age might have you thinking of the 70s as a decade of singular fashion, but the reality was even brighter and bolder than *Saturday Night Fever* would have you believe.

The baggy clothing of the hippie movement of the late 1960s bled into the decade that followed, while the long, conservative skirts of the 'New Look' from the 1940s were slashed and strapped into a new 'midi' form. Glam brought big hair and glitter. Disco brought big hair, open shirts and flares. It was also one of the last eras where fashion styles in both men and women were often unified, with fashion from across the globe adding all manner of new dimensions to the threads we wore.

BEAUTIFUL PEOPLE

Farrah Fawcett
`1976`

Farrah Fawcett's appearance on a Pro Arts Inc poster campaign in 1976, that sold 12 million copies worldwide, made her an instant sex symbol, while her role in hit show Charlie's Angels put her at the forefront of primetime style. Her hair, dubbed the 'Farrah Flick', became the look of the era, earning her a place among the decade's most influential women.

Bianca Jagger
`1971`

She may have shot to fame when she married the lead singer of the Rolling Stones in 1971, but Nicaragua-born Jagger made her impact on 70s fashion instantly, walking down the aisle in a white suit from Savile Row tailor Tommy Nutter. Jagger typified 70s individualism, wearing everything from suits to turbans, using her friendships with the designers of the era to model the latest fashions.

Debbie Harry
`1979`

While Heart Of Glass shattered charts in the final year of the decade, British singer Debbie Harry still made quite the impact on the fluid style of the 1970s. Tapping into the growing underground (and soon to be mainstream) punk movement that would rise to anarchic power in the 80s, Harry popularized a laid back and deconstructed look that took many an element from the fading disco era.

David Bowie
`1973`

David Bowie was a man of many faces, and each one left a lasting mark on fashion, music and pop culture. When Aladdin Sane arrived in 1973, its striking cover art – showing Bowie with a colorful lightning bolt across his face – became one of the most iconic images of the 20th century. Outside of his glam persona, Bowie's 70s style was a more formal affair, often favoring a gray suit with brown loafers.

Iman
`1976`

Few icons of the 70s had as much an impact on the fashion world and the mainstream as Iman. Designer Yves Saint Laurent once declared her his 'dream woman'. The Somali-American catwalk model shot to stardom with a highly publicized Vogue shoot in 1976 that cemented her status as a fashion trailblazer, as she helped reinvigorate high fashion. In 1992, she married fellow style icon David Bowie.

EARLY 70s

Much like any decade before and after it, the early years of the 1970s were heavily influenced by the styles and trends that informed the late 1960s. The hippie look was still all the rage, and as the 70s kicked off, all things tie-dye were very much in vogue. Along with homemade dyed clothing, an equally vibrant ethnic theme was making headlines in Western fashion. Capes as large as bedspreads, Mexican ponchos and Hungarian blouses were must-have items, with Moroccan-style designs and themes featuring heavily.

Hemlines were also a big talking point of the first few years of the decade, with the rise of the 'midi' skirt. The short skirt lengths of the 60s were out, with hemlines now dropped between the knee and the ankle. The 'Midi Look' even caused protests across the UK and North America, with fans of the miniskirt picketing stores stocking midi designs.

By 1971, designers and consumers were no longer on the same page, with long evening gowns and dresses becoming more of a casual item. Tailored items were also rising in popularity for both sexes, but by 1973 close-fitting clothes were making way for a far looser style.

Midi Look

In 1970, no look grabbed as many headlines and made as much of an impact on the fashion industry as the 'Midi Look'. The 1950s had seen formal, longer skirts holding sway before the arrival of the miniskirt in 1961. Hemlines above the knee held court among fashion designers and on retail shelves for most of the decade, but by the beginning of the 70s that was all about to change. While it actually first appeared around 1967, it was in 1970 that midi skirts really took off.

Hemlines were now more fluid, somewhere between the knee and the ankle. Rather than following the simple look of 1950s long skirts, the midi was often sashed, slashed or laced-up, offering a look that was both compact yet also had volume when in motion. Since it enhanced a small midriff and waist, it was very popular with thinner women. Maxi dresses were also becoming increasingly popular around the same time, with a similar design to the midi below the waist. However, while the miniskirt wasn't completely out of fashion (the popularity of knee-high boots helped keep it in style during the first few years of the decade), the rise of the midi even led some consumers to protest against shops that stocked them, often forming picket lines to deter other shoppers.

Glamour Wear

While the hippie look continued to remain popular in the early 1970s – serving as a progenitor to the individualism that would later typify the decade – glamour wear was fast becoming an equally adopted alternative. Glamour wear was a melting pot of styles and trends, often cherry-picked from years gone by and infused with a contemporary twist. Formal was made casual with dinner jackets (enhanced with large lapels, a calling card for both men and women in the 70s), which were then matched with bell-bottoms or other flared pants.

This early part of the decade was all about mixing and matching styles to create something new, fresh and exciting. Fitted blazers were teamed with tight-fitting jeans; flared pants were matched with skin-tight T-shirts. Every style had its place, from blouses to sweaters, with a noticeable crossover between the sexes. Accessories and shoes were just as eclectic, with everything from cloche hats to turbans making their way into both high-end fashion and high street combinations. Boots were also making a comeback, with go-go boots, crinkles and knee-highs all making a prolonged appearance.

Knitwear

Around 1972, heavyset knitwear began to make something of a comeback, with shetland, mohair and Norwegian-type styles appearing in both men and women's fashion. Knitted caps may have made way for light cloche designs, but by 1973 the knitting needle was king. Sweaters became the must-have item on both sides of the Atlantic. And these weren't just your regular sweaters – this was knitwear in myriad forms. Sweater dresses, sweater suits and sweater coats all made their way into eclectic wardrobes.

Not only did knitwear offer vast choices of color and style (everything from deep browns to light pastels), it also fed into the homemade ethos that bled into the decade from the tie-dye era of the 60s. Knitted items also worked well when paired with other clothing pieces, such as flared pants or shirts. Even when paired with outfits featuring plaids, stripes and flannels, knitwear remained a popular addition for both men and women. Fur was also in during the early 70s, so many sweaters were lined with real fur to add an extra style dimension. Big, chunky cardigans also proved a popular alternative, especially when paired with a large belt.

MID 70s

By 1974, and the onset of the midpoint of the decade, the Western fashion industry was struggling to find the next 'big thing'. The midi skirt may have been a success in certain regions, but overall it had been a PR nightmare that had caused many high street shops to close due to low sales. For a while, many men and women were simply happy to keep wearing the items that had come into fashion in the early years of the decade. Sweaters, tailored jackets and fitted jeans were all still making regular appearances in wardrobes across the world.

There were some significant changes, especially as the decade moved into 1975 and 1976. The T-shirt, long considered an underwear item to be worn beneath a shirt or blouse, was now considered an outer piece of clothing. This was the era when branded T-shirts, emblazoned with logos (including band names and symbols) made their mark, but it wasn't just a continued move towards full casual – dresses were also getting a makeover. Fashion designers were adopting 'the droop' in the mid-70s, where long dresses were loose, light and less clingy, tying into the continued popularity of capes and ponchos.

The t-shirt

The T-shirt, in various forms, had existed since the 19th century, where it was mainly used as an undergarment beneath a further layer of clothing. In fact, this trend continued right up until the beginning of the 1970s, where this simple garment suddenly found itself being worn as a top in its own right. Since the 70s was the era where crossover and unisex fashions were all the rage, the T-shirt fit this ethos perfectly.

Logos and brands were the real reason the T-shirt flourished from around 1974 onwards, embedding many of them into popular culture (so much so that many of the logos that found pop culture fame are still worn today). From the yellow 'have a nice day' face to the tongue and lips of The Rolling Stones, symbology became as important as style and color. It also became a popular means of both protest and advertising, with everything from Coca-Cola to the face of socialist revolutionary Che Guevera becoming hugely popular. Since it was such a simple casual item, both men and women could pair it with all manner of combinations, from denim (which was also finding a bigger following in the mid-70s) to tailored jackets.

Activewear

While we often associate the tracksuit (and the shell suit that followed) with the 1980s, it was actually during the mid-70s that the foundations of this trend were set in motion. 'Activewear' as it was generally known, was a trend predominantly favored by women, and ranged from one-piece jumpsuits to tank top/running short combos favored by track and field athletes during the mid 70s. Jumpsuits, originally used by parachuters and pilots, suddenly found themselves appearing in fashion designer toolkits, the one-piece nature of the design making it instantly popular with the growing shift towards casual clothing. As was the trend, the legs of a 70s jumpsuit were almost always flared, with myriad designs for the sleeves (ranging from long sleeves to none at all). Crop tops were also becoming a lot more popular for women at this time, as were tube tops, low-rise pants and hip-huggers. This move towards a more sporty, casual look saw a really noticeable drop in the use of accessories, but a rise in the popularity of items such as sweat headbands (inspired by tennis stars such as Björn Borg) and the use of trainers (or sneakers) outside of running/sports activities.

Punk

While we often think of the punk movement as an early 80s collision of music, fashion and political rebellion, it actually emerged and began to take shape deep in the 70s. It was around the mid-to-late 70s that the punk scene began to create a pocket of fashion that influenced both male and female styles. Vivienne Westwood and her partner Malcolm McLaren played a huge role in how punk evolved as its own trend and style, finding its roots in London before spreading across the Atlantic to the United States.

Much like the music that inspired it, punk fashion was brash, unapologetic and unlike anything else on the catwalks of the decade. Shirts, jeans and T-shirts were sometimes ripped or defaced with a symbol; tight drainpipe jeans were in, a defiant rebellion against the flares and bell-bottoms also doing the rounds; platforms were avoided in favor of simple Doc Martens or heavy-duty boots. Leather jackets were also a big thing during punk's early days, often enhanced with chains, spikes and patches – the ethos was to catch the eye, and offend it, if possible. Hairstyles were just as anti-establishment, with punks favoring shaved heads, spikes and mohawks over the longer styles of the day.

LATE 70s

As the 70s entered its twilight years, the fashion movements of designers and the high street continued to evolve. This was the time where all the styles of the 60s were forgotten as individualism began to shift in favor of more uniform looks. Sportswear continued to serve as a popular look outside of actual sport, and loose garments saw a move towards showing more skin. It was an era where the clothes and accessories were more about natural movement and the accentuation of shape. However, from the catwalk to the high street, the move towards a formal look was already in motion by 1978.

By 1979, the fashions we often think of when looking back to the 70s were fast transforming into those of the 1980s. Shoulder pads were in, as both men's and women's fashion began favoring a bulky look that accentuated the classic 'upside-down triangle'. These tailored jackets helped usher in a complete turnaround, as sportswear and casual wear were dropped in favor of formal attire. The 80s saw the suit become king (and queen), so the final year of the decade led to designers effectively getting a head start on the trends to come.

The 'Baggy' Look

Disco was still very much in vogue, thanks to the worldwide success of Saturday Night Fever, although fashions were beginning to fully shift towards the 'loose' look that took off in the mid 1970s. For women especially, when this push appeared around 1977, the focus on larger, looser and shapeless blouses and dresses caused a number of issues. Those with slimmer waists didn't want to have their size lost, while larger ladies were annoyed that these garments would make them look bigger.

For designers, the answer was simple: show more skin, but keep that loose mantra. More see-through materials began popping up, as did strapless designs and rolled up sleeves. Designers Calvin Klein and Bill Blass were leading the charge during '77 and '78, with their strappy/drawstring tops becoming must-have item for those looking to show off a little skin on the dancefloor or out and about. That bagginess also stretched to hair styles, which became far longer and less styled, aiming for a more natural look for both men and women. It affected accessories too, with scarves becoming the must-have addition to any loose fashion outfit.

Disco Look

It's impossible to discuss fashion in the 1970s without mentioning disco, the music phenomenon that inspired some of the most iconic fashion statements of the 20th century. These were clothes designed to work on the dancefloor, simultaneously showing off the body while offering the kind of material that would shine under the strobing lights of a disco mirrorball.

The emphasis was mainly on man-made materials such as Lycra and Spandex (tying into the increasing popularity of activewear). Wrap dresses were very popular among women, thanks to their light design and how they moved and swayed while dancing. For men, tailored suits with large lapels and open shirts were an instant hit thanks to John Travolta's iconic look in Saturday Night Fever.

For women, the disco look was about tying into the liberated tone of the music that inspired it. Clothing was about expressing femininity and sexuality, including everything from halterneck shirts to full-on ball gowns. For men, suits could be three-piece, or scaled back with a waistcoat. Ties, when used, were also much fatter and wider. Sunglasses, especially aviators, also became a must-have accessory for gentlemen looking to show their disco prowess on the dancefloor.

The Pantsuit

By 1979, fashion was once again in a state of metamorphosis, as it brought back the suited and booted look of the 1950s. After over a decade of popular fashions that swung towards all manner of casual looks, formal attire was preparing to make a comeback. Flared pants were becoming less and less common for both men and women, with the return of shoulder pads and other padded jackets signaling all manner of trends that would run rife in the decade to come. Business wear and casual wear were, effectively, merging into one.

The pantsuit become one of the most famous designs to emerge from this period, and one that's still worn and favored among women today. Pioneered by designer Yves Saint Laurent's famous 'Le Smoking' suit, the pantsuit become as much of a political statement for women in the workplace as it was a comfortable and flattering take on business wear. The idea was to take the male three-piece suit and enhance it, such as using a long, mid-length skirt and adding a slash to emphasis the legs, or wearing it with a ruffled shirt or heels.

STRETCH ARMSTRONG

Action figures had long been a staple of many a toy box but no child had ever seen or felt anything like Stretch Armstrong. At 15 inches, the trunk-wearing blond hunk toy was already large enough straight out of the box, but with a tug on his arms and legs he would become even bigger. Indeed, it was possible to stretch the fellow to as much as five feet, before letting go, allowing Armstrong to eventually shrink back to size.

The concept was created by Jesse D Horowitz, an employee at the US toy company Kenner, which was already well known for the Spirograph. Stretch Armstrong had a latex skin filled with a special ingredient: corn syrup that had been condensed by boiling. Entirely safe but prone to leaking if the toy was torn by pulling too far or too many times, it led to Kenner becoming the largest purchaser of corn syrup for the four years Stretch Armstrong was on sale.

One of the problems with this ingredient was that it would harden over time, making the toy much less stretchy. The latex skin would become thin, too. But by the time this happened, most kids would have got full value from the toy, having brutally contorted the body into all sorts of positions and experimented with the extent they could stretch it. It does mean that of the 40,000 toys that went into production at the time, very few exist. Yet one could be yours if your wallet will stretch that far.

▶ Stretch Armstrong arrived inside a huge box, laid flat within a Styrofoam coffin. Alongside the toy was a short instruction manual and a stretch mat, which could be laid out on the floor and used as a guide to see how far the toy could be pulled.

THE LEGACY

The original Stretch Armstrong was supplemented by a large number of versions intended for different international markets. Some were based on characters such as Donald Duck and the Incredible Hulk and they remained in production until 1980. In the 1990s, the toy was reissued sporting a t-shirt and shorts, and plans were made for a movie although they were later abandoned. Proving you can't put a good stretchable figure down, however, Netflix streamed a Stretch Armstrong animated series in 2017 and a comic has been released. New Stretch Armstrong toys can be bought today.

STRETCH ARMSTRONG

Bill Armasmith did a fine job of designing the toy's iconic look, and the smooth skin of the figure together with its well-defined muscle was initially achieved using ceramic molds. The head, meanwhile, was made of plastic and this was the only part of Armstrong that couldn't be stretched.

The boiled corn syrup mixture within Stretch Armstrong had some of the moisture removed from it, allowing a flowable gel to be produced. There is likely to have been other ingredients within the mix for greater viscosity. Its memory properties meant that it was able to recover and return to its original shape.

If Stretch became damaged, then kids could slap a bandage on him. There were ten of these in the box and the instructions detailed how they could be used for a repair. Very few of these exist in their loose form because so many would have been used at the time.

Information

Manufacturer: Kenner
First Released: 1976
Expect to pay: $1,000

© Alamy

BATTLESHIP

We don't like too many things that originated during times of conflict, but Battleship happens to be much more fun than getting shot. The naval battle game's origins are a little muddy but an early version named L'Attaque was popular in France during World War I. Most early versions of Battleship were played using paper and pen and went under different names, but the Battleship brand was established with Milton Bradley's plastic pegboard version.

Battleship is unlike most popular board games of the time, in that it relies more than most on hidden information. Instead of a single board that all players see, you have an individual space in which you track your own moves as well as your opponent's. This means that your initial attempts to bomb the enemy are always going to be complete guess work – the logic only comes in once you've registered a hit and can start hitting the surrounding spaces.

We tried all sorts of strategies when we were kids – lining the whole fleet up along one side of the board, and sticking solely to the outer edge. We placed ships at right angles to one another to confuse the opponent about ship length, and clustered most ships except the smallest together. However, while we'd often discover ways to beat the other kids, we never seemed to fool our parents – and it wasn't until much later that we realized they weren't strategic masterminds, they'd just conducted spy operations when we played with friends.

The lower board is used to track your own ships and your opponent's progress in blowing them up, while the pegs in the upright board are used to track your previous shots. The red pegs represent successful hits.

Information

Manufacturer: Milton Brac
First Released: 1967
Expect to pay: $3+

With five segments that need to be hit for a full destruction, the aircraft carrier is the largest piece in the game. Its placement has to be considered carefully because of the way it can block your other ships, and you'll hope your opponent doesn't manage to find it quickly.

A lot of older versions of the game used individual boards, but today it's more common for two players to share one board that folds out of either side of a central upright section – particularly if it's an electronic version that requires a computer, speakers and batteries.

THE LEGACY

Battleship was eventually computerized, meaning that you don't require a friend when you fancy a game, and 2008's Battleship Islands uses a grid of hexagonal tiles instead of squares to alter the strategy. The most improbable development was the film Battleship, which features a bizarre plot in which the United States Navy has to fight an alien fleet. Despite a budget of over $200 million and Liam Neeson's star power, the film struggled with critics and at the box office.

The plastic figures used to represent your ships haven't changed much over the years – these vintage versions are just about as detailed as the ones you'll find in Battleship games today. It's usually the board that is more complex, though the gameplay never changes.

SONY WALKMAN

Information
Manufacturer: Sony
First Released: 1979
Expect to pay: $400+

The Walkman has gone from a music revolution (a revolution that Sony even called out in its advertising campaign) to a cultural icon. The Walkman is the device that had millions of teens creating their own mixtapes of tracks and sharing them with friends. It's the product used in modern films to date flashback sequences or time-travel sections. And it's the device that kick-started the portable music industry.

Before the Walkman, the only way to listen to music on the go was with a portable radio, playing one of a small number of standard music stations. Cassettes changed all of that, and allowed users to customize their listening experience with their favorite albums and artists. Enjoying your own music outside of your home was an exciting prospect, and Sony made sure to put the focus on the device's potential.

The Japanese company advertised the Walkman as a culturally definitive product, but one that was incredibly personal thanks to the ability to create your own playlists. For Sony, it was the best of both worlds – they created a mass-market product that still felt unique to each individual. The Walkman was incredibly popular with teens, appearing in some of the most iconic movies, including *The Terminator*, *Back To The Future* and James Bond film *A View To A Kill*.

The brand lived on though MP3 players and music-focused phones until 2015, when Sony replaced the Walkman app on its own-branded smartphones with an app simply called 'Music'.

The Hotline button reduced the volume of the music slightly and if you spoke into the microphone on the Walkman, the other listener would hear you through their headphones, over the music.

THE LEGACY

Launched in 1992, Sony's MiniDisc player/recorder was the first serious successor to the Walkman, but the format never really took off. Soon, though, digital music took over, with MP3 players like Apple's iPod allowing users to store thousands of songs in a device smaller than a Walkman. Nowadays, most music fans either store songs on their smartphones, or stream music over the internet through services like Spotify.

Dual headphone jacks meant two people could listen to the music at the same time – as long as they had their own pair of headphones.

SONY
STEREO CASSETTE PLAYER TPS-L2

STEREO

MIC

STOP EJECT

LEFT RIGHT VOLUME

DC IN 3V

SONY

The number of cassette tapes you could carry was the only limit on your portable music collection. As well as buying prerecorded albums, you could compile your own mixtapes.

The Walkman didn't need much power, and required just one AA battery. It could also be powered via the DC In jack if you didn't have a battery handy.

© Argos/Alamy

MUSIC IN THE 70s

From Abba to The Sex Pistols, from heavy metal to disco, we chronicle the decade's invaluable contribution to music history

The 1970s were an era of musical innovation and evolution. They shook up the establishment with the explosion of punk, filled the dancefloors with the rise of disco, gave birth to heavy metal, hip hop and glam rock, giving us unforgettable riffs, pioneering breakbeats, and gloriously ostentatious stage personas doused in glitter and glam. They gave us solo icons: the piano-pounding brilliance of Elton John, the evolution of David Bowie from glam rock alter-ego to crafter of pop-krautrock, the superstar presence of iconic divas Gloria Gaynor and Diana Ross. Iconic groups rolled out the hit singles, Abba and Queen leading the pack with their uncanny ability to create one chart success after another. It was an era that gave us controversy, from Donna Summer's provocative moans to the scandal of the Sex Pistols' public profanity and lyrical lashing of the institution of monarchy. In contrast to the political content in the music of acts like Sex Pistols, The Clash and Bob Marley, this was also a decade when music offered fun and escapism in the shape of groups like Kiss and the Village People. It was the decade in which the world caught Saturday Night Fever, catapulting the Bee Gees to fame, where pop-friendly rockers like Slade and Fleetwood Mac topped the charts, Pink Floyd and Blondie experimented with new sounds and styles, and Black Sabbath rocked us in ways we'd never heard before. It's no coincidence that albums from likes of Elton, Fleetwood and Floyd remain some of the best-selling of all time. It's a sign that the music of this decade was not only definitive for that generation, but for the generations indebted to its legacy.

EVENTS

The Beatles break up

April 1970

The 1970s began with the huge news that the most famous and, arguably, most influential band of all time was breaking up. It was the end of an era, but the end of an era necessarily means the start of a new one. In that sense, while the breakup may have broken the hearts of The Beatles' fans, it also cleared the way for new artists to take center stage and create their own history.

700,000 people visit the Isle of Wight

August 1970

An estimated 600,000-700,000 descended on an island with a usual population of just 100,000 for this event. The festival lasted for five days, but its legacy lived on in the many live recordings and in influencing one of its attendees, Michael Eavis, to start the Glastonbury Festival.

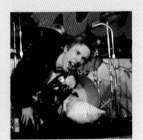

God Save The Queen scandalizes the nation

May 1977

The fear that the British establishment felt when confronted with the rebellious movement that was punk was perhaps best encapsulated by the response to the Sex Pistols' 1977 single *God Save The Queen*. The BBC refused to play the song, considering it too provocative.

Saturday Night Fever released

December 1977

Saturday Night Fever was a cultural phenomenon that harnessed the momentum of the burgeoning genre of disco and cemented its place in the mainstream. With an iconic soundtrack headlined by Bee Gees hits, the film helped kick the disco craze into gear and making it a defining sound of the decade.

Michael Jackson goes solo

August 1979

Michael Jackson was already a star thanks to his work as part of the Jackson 5, but with the release of *Off The Wall*, he announced his arrival as a solo performer. In retrospect, we now know what a huge moment Jackson's move to solo work was, starting his rise to becoming one of the biggest stars in music history.

POP ICONS

The 70s gave us some of pop music's most enduring performers and a host of iconic songs that are instantly recognizable to this day. Pop glam rockers like Slade and Mud delivered big hits, while teen-friendly acts like the Bay City Rollers and The Osmonds thrilled armies of screaming young fans. When it comes to evaluating the pop music of the era, though, there are two acts that stand head and shoulders above the rest when it comes to their profile and success: Abba and Elton John. After winning Eurovision in 1974, Abba took Europe by storm, delivering a string of classic number one hits such as *Waterloo*, *Mamma Mia*, *Take A Chance On Me*, *Knowing Me, Knowing You* and *Dancing Queen*. Elton John, meanwhile, drew on a variety of musical styles, mixing pop and rock to create a slew of classic hits. Indeed, the 1970s was a strong decade for acts that straddled the boundary between pop and rock. Queen, Fleetwood Mac and David Bowie are all examples of rock acts that incorporated a strong pop sensibility into their music, achieving huge commercial and critical success.

▲ **Abba**

Sweden's most successful musical act was formed in 1972. Their 1974 Eurovision Contest win helped bring them to the attention of the European public. The group enjoyed success in the wake of that with songs like *Mamma Mia* and *SOS*. With the release of their greatest hits album and new single *Fernando* in 1976, however, the group's popularity exploded. The string of iconic hits that followed and their near-constant presence at the top of the charts for the rest of the decade made them one of the defining acts of the era.

GREATEST HITS ALBUMS

Greatest Hits
Abba
1976

The album that catapulted Abba to superstardom was, ironically, given that they'd yet to fully hit their stride outside of their native Sweden, their *Greatest Hits* album. The record included classics like *SOS*, *I Do, I Do, I Do, I Do, I Do*, *Mamma Mia*, *Waterloo*, and the single that had just hit number one in the UK at the time, *Fernando*. The following year, Abba released their *Arrival* album, which launched *Dancing Queen* as the number one song in the US.

The Singles 1969-1973
The Carpenters
1973

The brother/sister duo that were the Carpenters were a huge act in both the US and UK in the 1970s, so much so that this album was one of the best-selling released in the decade. The album collected together the duo's biggest hits, including *Rainy Days And Mondays*, *For All We Know* and *Superstar*.

Goodbye Yellow Brick Road
Elton John
1973

Elton John was incredibly prolific in the 1970s, but this record stands out thanks to the important role it played making him a global superstar and its recognition to this day as one of his best. It also included the first version of his most famous song, *Candle In The Wind*.

Grease: The Original Soundtrack From The Motion Picture
Various
1978

The hit film *Grease* was a phenomenon and the album is not only one of the best-selling soundtrack albums of all time, but one of the best-selling albums full stop.

Here Come The Warm Jets
Brian Eno
1974

Pop music can often be written off as shallow, commercial and unimportant. Brian Eno's experimental, avant-garde approach to making pop music with this record flew in the face of that snobbery. It's a great example of the way Eno experimented with pushing pop music forward in the '70s.

▲ Elton John

In the early years of the 70s, Elton John began to build an audience for his trademark blend of sweeping ballads and big rock-infused epics. In 1973, number one albums *Don't Shoot Me I'm Only The Piano Player* and *Goodbye Yellow Brick Road* made him a worldwide star, introducing us to songs like *Crocodile Rock*, *Bennie And the Jets* and *Candle In The Wind*. John would gain a reputation for spectacular stage costumes that included sparkles, ostrich feathers and gigantic light-up glasses, as he continued to churn out the hits.

▲ Fleetwood Mac

The early years of the 1970s were a time of chaos for Fleetwood Mac. Their line-up frequently changed and they faced legal battles when their manager claimed he owned the Fleetwood Mac name and started up his own fake band. Though they had some success in this early period, it was in 1975 with the release of the band's self-titled album that Fleetwood Mac really broke through into the mainstream. The band followed up in 1977 with the hugely successful *Rumours*, which included classics like *Go Your Own Way*, *Dreams* and *Don't Stop*.

SONGS

My Sharona
The Knack
1979

With its catchy guitar hook and memorable stuttering vocals, this power pop anthem became the song of the summer in 1979. Unfortunately for the band that created and performed it, The Knack, they would prove to be one-hit wonders.

Bye Bye Baby
Bay City Rollers
1975

Originally a hit for The Four Seasons in 1965, teeny-bopper act the Bay City Rollers released their own version of *Bye Bye Baby* ten years later. The single sold a million copies and was the best-selling single in the UK for 1975.

Puppy Love
Donny Osmond
1972

The original version of *Puppy Love* was recorded by Paul Anka in 1960, but the most famous version of the song is unquestionably the cover performed by teen idol Donny Osmond, released in 1972. It was one of many hits Donny and other Osmond family members would create in the 70s.

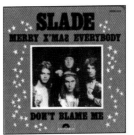

Merry Xmas Everybody
Slade
1973

The fact that we all hear this Christmas classic every year when the festive season rolls around tells you all you need to know about it. It was far from Slade's only hit in the 1970s, but it is the one that they will forever be known for.

Go Your Own Way
Fleetwood Mac
1976

The first single from Fleetwood Mac's *Rumours*, *Go Your Own Way* documented the strained relationship between band members Stevie Nicks and Lindsey Buckingham. Things might not have been rosy within the band, but this single catapulted them to new levels of stardom and made the album it was taken from a monster smash.

ROCK

The 1970s took rock music in all kinds of exciting new directions, delivering a diverse range of styles and laying the foundations for the evolution of the genre for years to come. The Eagles took the world by storm with their best-selling album *Hotel California*, and Queen, formed in 1970, churned out hit after hit with songs like *Bohemian Rhapsody, We Will Rock You* and *We Are The Champions*, while performing to huge crowds, such as the record 150,000 that came to see them play Hyde Park in 1976. The 1970s also gave birth to a harder, riff-led style of rock that would come to be known as heavy metal. The vanguard of this new style was led by pioneers Black Sabbath, Led Zeppelin and Deep Purple. Then there was the glittery, glitzy style of glam rock, perhaps best embodied by David Bowie's transformation into Ziggy Stardust, which would come to help define the sound and fashion of the decade. As the decade went on, bands like AC/DC, Kiss and Van Halen would take influence from the likes of Sabbath, Zeppelin and Bowie, continuing to take rock in new directions.

ICONS

▲ **David Bowie**

You could argue about whether David Bowie should really be considered a "rock" act or not, but that difficulty in classifying his work is one of the keys to his enduring success. He released a host of classic albums during the 70s, including *Hunky Dory*, the glam-infused *The Rise And Fall Of Ziggy Stardust* and *Diamond Dogs*. Bowie continued to evolve in the second half of the decade, moving to Berlin and taking influences from the scene there before creating *Low* and *Heroes*, famous for its iconic track of the same name.

GREATEST HITS ALBUMS

Led Zeppelin IV

Led Zeppelin

1971

Showcasing their ability to blend blues, folk and rock, Led Zeppelin's untitled album, generally known as *Led Zeppelin IV*, is one of the most influential and successful rock albums of all time. It includes many of the band's most famous songs, including *Stairway To Heaven* and *Black Dog*.

The Rise And Fall Of Ziggy Stardust And The Spiders From Mars

David Bowie

1972

The ever-evolving David Bowie created one of his most iconic looks and musical creations when he took on the persona of glam rock star Ziggy Stardust. The single *Starman* helped propel the album to huge success.

Hotel California

Eagles

1976

With over 32 million copies sold, there's little argument to be made about the Eagles' *Hotel California* album being one of the most important released in the '70s. Its iconic track of the same name, *Hotel California*, was written first, with the rest of the album based on the themes in that song.

Highway To Hell

AC/DC

1979

AC/DC had already released five albums by the time *Highway To Hell* came out in 1979, but it was this record that raised their profile to a new level and sent new fans scurrying back to find their older work. The band would have a huge influence on the heavy metal music to follow.

Sticky Fingers

The Rolling Stones

1971

The Rolling Stones may have been at the peak of their success in the 1960s, but they were still producing great music in the 1970s. Indeed, this album, which includes *Brown Sugar* and *Wild Horses*, is still considered to be one of their best.

▲ Kiss

With their painted faces, outrageous costumes and stage shows that included pyrotechnics and levitating drum kits, Kiss were arguably the ultimate expression of the glam trend that swept the 70s, making their performances as much about the spectacle as they were the music. Nevertheless, the band still delivered plenty of hits, including *Detroit Rock City*, *I Was Made For Lovin' You* and *Rock And Roll All Nite*. They sold out huge concerts and became a merchandise machine selling Kiss dolls, lunchboxes, comics and even a pinball machine.

▲ Queen

Led by iconic frontman Freddie Mercury and fluffy-haired guitar legend Brian May, Queen will forever be remembered as music legends thanks to the string of successes they enjoyed in the 70s. The sheer number of singalong classics they churned out is breathtaking: *Bohemian Rhapsody*, *Another One Bites The Dust* and *Don't Stop Me Now*, to name a few. Their iconic look, record-breaking sales, and their gifts to sports fans, in the form of terrace anthems *We Are The Champions* and *We Will Rock You*, ensure their legendary status.

Paranoid

Black Sabbath

1970

The first single from the album of the same name helped to catapult Black Sabbath and their charismatic frontman Ozzy Osbourne to fame. This pioneering heavy metal hit played a vital role in influencing the evolution of the genre throughout the rest of the decade.

Bohemian Rhapsody

Queen

1975

Conventional wisdom suggested that this six-minute chorus-free epic that wandered through ballad, opera and hard rock styles was too long and too strange to get the radio play it would need to be a hit. Conventional wisdom isn't always right; Queen topped the charts for nine weeks and sold more than a million copies in three months.

Rock And Roll All Nite

Kiss

1975

This catchy tune is the definitive Kiss song, so much so that the band used it to close all their shows from 1976 onwards. The original version wasn't actually that big a hit, but the band soon followed up with a live version of the song that quickly stormed the charts.

Overkill

Motorhead

1979

This driving metal hit is the archetypal Motorhead song, combining elements of heavy metal and punk to deliver a speedy, riff-heavy classic. It was a sound influenced by the work of other bands in the decade, but was also definitively Motorhead's own.

Smoke On The Water

Deep Purple

1973

The riff that forms that backbone of Deep Purple's most famous song has to be one of the most instantly recognizable in all of music history. Anyone who has tried to learn to play guitar has probably tried their hand at it thanks to its simplicity.

PUNK & NEW WAVE

Partly emerging as a rejection of the perceived pretension and excess expressed in glam and prog rock, punk responded with a brash new style defined by its attitude as much as by its stripped-down, speedy sound. Indeed, punk was far more than a musical style. It was about a DIY approach, an insistence that anyone could be in a band by playing simple three-chord tunes instead of fiddly and complex guitar solos, and an anti-establishment political ethos. Led by the success of bands like the Sex Pistols, The Clash and the Buzzcocks, the genre emerged from the underground to become a phenomenon in 1977. Green-haired, leather-clad punks became a common sight on the streets, creating panic in an establishment that felt threatened by this youthful rebellion. Punk was also notable for being more open to women than the male-dominated realms of rock and metal.

▶ Sex Pistols

When you think of punk, you think of the Sex Pistols. More than any other band, this quartet composed of Johnny Rotten, Steve Jones, Paul Cook and Glen Matlock (later replaced by Sid Vicious), were responsible for the explosion of punk. Rising to infamy thanks to a notorious TV appearance where they swore at host Bill Grundy, they became public enemy number one for the tabloid press, leading to a host of canceled shows. This only served to enhance their anti-establishment reputation, making them punk's biggest band. Despite quickly burning out and releasing only one album, they are punk's most influential act.

ICONS

▲ The Clash

The Clash created two of punk's greatest albums in the 1970s, the self-titled *The Clash* and *London Calling*. The band blended the politics, attitude and a rough edge that characterized other punk bands with a greater willingness to experiment with their sound, which would become a feature of the post-punk and new wave bands that emerged at the end of the decade. The strained but productive partnership between lead vocalist Joe Strummer and lead guitarist Mick Jones produced some of the decade's most famous punk anthems in *White Riot*, *London's Burning* and *London Calling*.

▲ Blondie

Blondie were one of the most successful new wave bands that arose in the tail end of the 1970s. They started their career as a punk band, but found more success when they began experimenting to incorporate other styles. Their definitive album was *Parallel Lines*, released in 1978. The record included elements of reggae, pop and disco, filtered through their earlier punk sound. It featured a number of successful singles including *Call Me*, *Rapture*, *The Tide Is High* and arguably their most famous song, *Heart Of Glass*.

GREATEST HITS ALBUMS

Ramones
Ramones
1976

Before punk hit its stride in the UK, a handful of American bands pioneered the sound, none more so than the Ramones. Their self-titled debut album, which included *Blitzkrieg Bop* and *Judy Is A Punk*, laid down a template for the many punk bands that would follow.

London Calling
The Clash
1979

The Clash's most critically acclaimed album is the perfect example of the band's eclectic and creative approach to punk. You can hear the influence of reggae, ska, lounge jazz, rockabilly and more in a track list that includes *Death Or Glory*, *Brand New Cadillac*, *Rudie Can't Fail* and *The Guns Of Brixton*.

The Feeding Of The 5000
Crass
1979

At a time where punk was already, depending on your perspective, fading from prominence or evolving into something new, Crass released an album that doubled down on punk's roots. Its raw, aggressive sound and expression of anarchist politics came at you like a slap in the face.

The Scream
Siouxsie And The Banshees
1978

Though they had a reputation in and emerged out of the UK punk scene, Siouxsie And The Banshees are credited as one of the innovators of the post-punk sound that would move beyond it with this album. It was received as a landmark record due to its experimental approach and proved to be highly influential.

Unknown Pleasures
Joy Division
1979

Joy Division's debut album was not a huge success at the time, at least in part due to the fact that no singles were released from the album. However, the reputation of the record has grown over the years and it is now regarded as a vital and influential part of music history.

SONGS

God Save The Queen
Sex Pistols
1977

The Sex Pistols' most famous song was incredibly controversial at the time of its release, with the BBC refusing to play it due to its comparison of the Queen with a "fascist regime". It became a powerful symbol of the punk movement's anti-establishment credentials.

New Rose
The Damned
1976

Coming out a matter of weeks before the Sex Pistols' *Anarchy In The UK*, The Damned's *New Rose* is often credited as being the UK's first punk single. It represents the moment punk truly marked itself out from its progenitors and began to be acknowledged as a unique genre of its own in the UK.

Heart Of Glass
Blondie
1979

This mega-hit will forever be the song with which Blondie is most strongly associated. Its blending of disco with rock and its innovative use of electronic drum machines and synthesizers gave it a unique sound that would influence electronic and synth musicians that would follow in the 80s.

Boys Don't Cry
The Cure
1979

Before they would come to be associated with goth rock, The Cure were associated with the post-punk and new wave scene. Their classic single *Boys Don't Cry* announced them to the world with that catchy guitar line and singer Robert Smith's distinctive vocal style.

Damaged Goods
Gang Of Four
1978

Released through indie label Fast Product, Gang Of Four's *Damaged Goods* was such a hit that it got the band signed to EMI. It was a great example of how post-punk artists were able to inject punk with a more pop-friendly sensibility.

DISCO & FUNK

Disco and funk both had their roots in the urban American nightlife of the 1960s. It wasn't until the 1970s, however, when disco and funk hit the peak of their popularity. Picking up on the funk pioneers of the 60s, artists like Sly and the Family Stone, Kool & The Gang, Chaka Khan and Stevie Wonder took the bassline-led grooves of the genre to the radio and the attention of the masses. Disco enjoyed a similar, but more rapid rise, exploding suddenly in the mid-70s with a series of chart topping hits from the likes of Carl Douglas, Gloria Gaynor, KC And The Sunshine Band, Donna Summer and the Bee Gees. Both genres encouraged people to take to the dancefloor and party in contrast to more introspective or aggressive genres that were popular in the decade, such as prog rock and punk. Disco in particular was seen as an escapist genre, offering people a respite from the economic problems that plagued the decade. Funk continued to evolve into the 80s, but disco would be defined by the decade in which it rose to prominence. Almost as quickly as it arose, a backlash saw it quickly wane in popularity in 1979 and fizzle out in the early 1980s.

ICONS

▲ Bee Gees

The falsetto voice of Barry Gibb, working in combination with the harmonies of his brothers Robin and Maurice, is one of the defining sounds of disco. The group had their first success in the 60s but their popularity had waned by the mid-70s. It was during this period that the group turned to disco and Barry found his trademark falsetto sound. The true turning point, however, was when the Bee Gees penned many classic tunes for movie *Saturday Night Fever*. They rocketed to superstardom, netting a string of number ones and multiple awards.

GREATEST HITS ALBUMS

Love To Love You Baby

Donna Summer

1975

Donna Summer's second album was her first to be released worldwide. Summer's sexual moaning on the title track made it a controversial song, but won her plenty of attention. The success of the song and album put her on the path to becoming 'The Queen of Disco'.

There's A Riot Goin' On

Sly And The Family Stone

1971

With *There's A Riot Goin' On*, Sly And The Family Stone took a darker and more conceptual approach than you might expect from a genre associated with being upbeat. However, that experimental approach means it is now seen as an important funk classic.

Mothership Connection

Parliament

1975

Funk legends Parliament's bizarre concept album themed around space travel and UFOs is known as one of the band's best. It not only sold well at the time, but also has been retrospectively recognized for having a huge influence on funk, rock, jazz and dance music.

Saturday Night Fever

Various

1977

The soundtrack for blockbuster film *Saturday Night Fever* is significant for a number of reasons. Not only did it introduce us to a number of disco classics, it gave birth to the incarnation of the Bee Gees we now know, and took disco to its highest point of popularity.

Off The Wall

Michael Jackson

1979

Before he became "The King of Pop", Michael Jackson released this classic disco record. Songs like *Don't Stop 'Til You Get Enough* and *Rock With You* helped win the record a lot of praise and helped Jackson step away from The Jackson 5 and forge his own path.

▲ Donna Summer

Known as 'The Queen of Disco', Donna Summer is truly a disco idol. She started off with success in Europe with her first album, *Lady Of The Night*, before the success of the single *Love To Love You Baby* in the US brought her to the attention of the wider world. In 1977 she truly arrived on the scene as a certified disco star. She had great success with the albums *I Remember Yesterday* and *Once Upon A Time* and hit number one in the UK with her single *I Feel Love*. By the end of the decade, she had become a cultural icon.

▲ KC And The Sunshine Band

KC And The Sunshine Band were a group that melded elements of funk and disco to create a collection of hit tunes that would invariably, to use their own words, make you want to "shake your booty". As well as that song – *Shake Your Booty* – the band are known for *That's The Way*, *I'm Your Boogie Man*, *Get Down Tonight*, *Keep It Comin' Love* and *Boogie Shoes*. This impressive list of chart successes made them an ever-present sound in the disco and funk era.

♫ SONGS

Superstition
Stevie Wonder

`1972`

Music legend Stevie Wonder is perhaps best known for this soul-tinged funk classic. Legend goes that fellow musician Jeff Beck came up with the opening beat and Stevie improvised almost the whole song, including its classic riff, over the top of it.

Stayin' Alive
Bee Gees

`1977`

Hear this track and you think of John Travolta's famous dance moves from *Saturday Night Fever*. The two go hand-in-hand. It is undoubtedly the Bee Gees' most famous song, and one of the most recognizable songs of all time.

YMCA
Village People

`1978`

When it comes to singalongs, it doesn't get much easier than *YMCA*. That simplicity, along with the song's light-hearted feel and famous hand-movement dance have all helped to make the Village People's biggest song into a disco classic that everyone knows.

I Will Survive
Gloria Gaynor

`1978`

Gloria Gaynor's powerful performance and the song's lyrics about enduring in the face of adversity have led to it being adopted as a symbol of women's strength and as an LGBTQ anthem. It's also just a great song, hence why it has sold 14 million copies.

Jungle Boogie
Kool & The Gang

`1973`

What song better captures the way funk makes you want to take to the dancefloor than Kool & The Gang's infectious single *Jungle Boogie*? The song has had a long life, being sampled by the Beastie Boys, Madonna and Janet Jackson, as well as appearing in Quentin Tarantino film *Pulp Fiction*.

ALTERNATIVE

The musical landscape of today owes a lot to the 70s. The decade gave birth to many new genres and was the era when several evolving ones came into prominence. Some of them had their heyday in the decade, as with punk and disco, but some of them have become an indelible and permanent fixture in mainstream music culture. We are talking about the birth of hip hop in the music of artists like Grandmaster Flash and The Sugarhill Gang, the mainstream success of reggae led by Bob Marley, the evolution of prog rock at the hands of bands and artists such as Pink Floyd and Mike Oldfield, the new heights hit by R&B thanks to legends like Diana Ross, the pioneers of Afrobeat like Fela Kuti, and the transformation of ska at the hands of the two-tone movement. These artists not only left their mark on that decade with the music they created, but also on the music we listen to today.

▶ Bob Marley

Nobody did more to popularize reggae than the icon that is Bob Marley, bringing the sound of Jamaica to the attention of the globe and becoming one of the best-selling artists of all time in the process. Along with The Wailers, he put out a host of brilliant albums including *Catch A Fire*, *Burnin'*, *Natty Dread* and *Exodus*, and a parade of classic tunes such as *Stir It Up*, *Get Up, Stand Up*, *I Shot The Sheriff*, *Jamming*, *One Love* and *No Woman, No Cry*.

ICONS

▲ Pink Floyd

Pink Floyd were prog rock pioneers that changed music through their experimentation in the recording studio, elaborate, wandering compositions and their epic stage shows that included giant floating pigs and 40-foot cardboard walls. They are best known for producing one of the most critically acclaimed and best-selling albums of all time, *Dark Side Of The Moon*, but also gave us *Wish You Were Here*, *Animals* and *The Wall* in the same decade. Their huge commercial success and far-reaching musical influence makes them one of the most iconic bands in music history.

▲ The Sugarhill Gang

Before Jay-Z and Eminem, before the gangster rap of NWA, before the wars between Biggie and Tupac, came one of the originators of hip hop: The Sugarhill Gang. The group is credited with releasing the first rap single to hit the top 40 in the US with *Rapper's Delight*. That achievement is significant enough, but the group did far more than that for the burgeoning genre. They also formed the Sugar Hill record label and signed other important hip hop pioneers like Grandmaster Flash And The Furious Five, The Sequence and Funky 4 + 1.

GREATEST HITS
ALBUMS

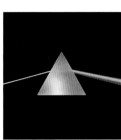

Exodus
Bob Marley & The Wailers
`1977`

In 1976 Bob Marley moved from Jamaica to England where he would produce one of his greatest albums: *Exodus*. The record stayed in the album charts for 56 weeks in a row and contained hit singles *Exodus, Waiting In Vain, Jamming* and *One Love*.

Dark Side Of the Moon
Pink Floyd
`1973`

Songs bleed into one another with a hypnotic, dreamlike character on *Dark Side Of The Moon*, while strange, disconnected sounds emerge out of the ether to feed into its overarching philosophical concepts exploring human life. You might think that would make it too experimental to be a success, but it was just too good to be anything but.

Zombie
Fela Kuti
`1976`

Though this album was released in the UK, it was far bigger in Fela Kuti's native Nigeria where it resulted in a violent backlash from the Nigerian government thanks to its political lyrics. It is now recognized as an incredibly influential record that laid the foundations for the Afrobeat music of today.

Tubular Bells
Mike Oldfield
`1973`

Mike Oldfield's experimental prog rock album was a surprising global success that launched Virgin Records, a label that would itself go on to have an important influence on 70s music. The album owes much of its success to the profile it gained when its intro was used as the iconic theme of hit horror film *The Exorcist*.

Handsworth Revolution
Steel Pulse
`1978`

Reggae will forever be associated with its homeland of Jamaica, but Birmingham outfit Steel Pulse and their debut album *Handsworth Revolution* took the sound of Jamaica and helped evolve it in the UK and eventually the US. This critical and commercial success led to a tour alongside Bob Marley in the year of its release.

SONGS

The Carpet Crawlers
Genesis
`1975`

Genesis are now best-known for the Phil Collins-led era that brought them huge success in the 80s and 90s, but before that, Genesis were one of prog rock's most important bands and this song is just one example of that.

A Message To You, Rudy
The Specials
`1979`

The West Midlands in the 1970s was an incubator for a new brand of music influenced by ska, reggae and punk, birthing a new strain of ska known as two-tone. The Specials were one of its most famous proponents and this song one of its first huge hits.

Rapper's Delight
The Sugarhill Gang
`1979`

If you're looking for the moment that hip hop burst on to the scene, you need look no further than the release of The Sugarhill Gang's *Rapper's Delight*. The onset of that catchy bassline was the beginning of a new movement that owes a huge debt to this song.

Rappin & Rocking The House
Funky 4 + 1
`1979`

Funky 4 + 1 are credited with a number of firsts: the first hip hop group to get a recording deal, the first group to have a female MC, Sha-Rock, and the first to perform on national TV. *Rappin & Rocking The House* was their first single.

Ain't No Mountain High Enough
Diana Ross
`1970`

As if she didn't do enough for music in the 1960s with The Supremes, Diana Ross proved that there was indeed no mountain high enough for her as she kicked off her legendary solo career with *Ain't No Mountain High Enough*, her first solo number one.

143